SUCCESSFUL
COMPOSITE
TECHNIQUES

SUCCESSFUL COMPOSITE TECHNIQUES

A practical introduction to the use of modern composite materials

Keith Noakes

OSPREY

Published in 1989 by Osprey Publishing Limited
59 Grosvenor Street, London W1X 9DA

Osceola, Wisconsin 54020, USA

Sole distributors in the USA

British Library Cataloguing in Publication Data

Noakes, Keith
    Successful composite techniques.
    1. Composite materials
    I. Title
    620.1'18

ISBN 0-85045-877-3

Editor Ian Penberthy
Design Gwyn Lewis

Front cover photograph and
back cover illustration by kind
permission of Ferrari CEFAC
SpA

Filmset and printed in England by
BAS Printers Limited, Over Wallop, Hampshire

Contents

Introduction

This book is intended as an introduction and guide to modern composites and will outline their processing methods. It is aimed at those considering their use, or wishing to obtain an understanding of the basic materials and their processing methods.

The term 'modern composites', used throughout this book, covers the use of resins in conjunction with a range of man-made fibres, such as glass, carbon and Kevlar. The book includes descriptions of these materials in their various forms, together with explanations of why and where they are used. It also describes a variety of processing methods, including the tooling and equipment required.

As the book is intended as a basic instructional guide, the text will refer to materials in general and, therefore, will avoid the use of trade names where possible.

In addition to serving as a guide to the use of modern composites, this book will also cover some basic design steps.

Composite structures, in various forms, have been used for hundreds of years. Technically, composite means a combination of materials; early ships would have used combinations of wood and metal, as would early aircraft and cars. However, as already mentioned, this book covers materials described as *modern* composites.

A large percentage of modern composite technology is based on the use of some form of fibre, which is formed into structural materials by the use of matrix resins that bind the individual fibres together. The performance of the finished structure will depend on the potential performance of the fibre, the resin and the way in which these two materials are combined.

The potential material performance has led, over many years, to the availability of a very wide range of man-made fibres to meet required performance levels. The resin technologists have also produced an equally wide range of matrix-resin systems. This combination has given designers in composites the opportunity to reach an exciting, advanced level of engineering in entirely new materials.

But how new is new? Although in recent years, composites have become important structural materials in aerospace and automotive applications, equally advanced structural use was made of composite materials many years ago. One excellent example is the use of a composite material, called Gordon Aerolite, to produce a Spitfire fuselage during World War 2.

Gordon Aerolite was developed in Britain by a company called Duxford Aero Research, later to become part of the composite manufacturing company CIBA-GEIGY. This material consisted of flax (linen) fibres impregnated with phenolic resin. The resin could be formed in a mould and was cured under pressure at an elevated temperature. This method enabled accurate components to be manufactured, and their structural performance levels were of great interest to designers.

At one stage of the war, it was feared that a shortage of aluminium was imminent, so a fuselage for the British-built Supermarine Spitfire was designed to utilize the new material. Although this developed fuselage was never to fly (the supply of aluminium never ran out), the finished structure did meet static performance levels and was a potential alternative to aluminium. This must rate as one of the earliest, if not the first, primary structures to be designed utilizing resin-impregnated fibres.

The first widespread use of fibre-and-resin technology took place in the early 1950s, when glass fibre and polyester resins became available. The versatility, and comparatively simple methods of use, of this combination soon led to its appearance in boats, car bodywork, and many industrial applications. This form of glass-fibre work is still very widely used, but has been overshadowed by the structural capabilities of materials such as carbon, Kevlar, and other fibres, coupled with the high performance of other resin systems.

The penalty, however, is that these later, hi-tech materials and methods are much more expensive and require greater skill levels. Despite these apparent disadvantages, massive strides have been taken to advance modern composite materials in a wide range of applications and industries.

The aerospace industry must take a large amount of the credit for composite technology advances. There are several reasons for this: weight saving, mechanical performance, versatility of manufacture, etc. Also, and very important to the advancement of any technology, are the preset performance requirements laid down in the many specifications. This leads to the composite materials manufacturers striving to meet these performance requirements.

On the other hand are the race-car manufacturers, who require low-weight, high-mechanical-performance components, but are not restricted by preset performance specifications. Therefore, they can develop techniques at a faster pace.

These two industries have been responsible for the giant steps taken in the development of composite technology, although many other industries have contributed to its development, too. Many more are now utilizing the vast range of available composite materials and techniques.

Shown here is an example of composite use in the manufacture of sports goods

The range of materials and techniques is now very wide but, in many cases, processing requirements, that is, the equipment and the level of required skills, will limit the choice. Both these points can be achieved, however, where the requirement is justified from the aspects of cost or time to learn.

This book will outline the processing methods and equipment requirements, giving the reader an understanding of the technology and sufficient knowledge to manufacture something.

The versatility of composite construction is so wide that those who can benefit from its capability range from the individual working at home to the large volume producer. Versatility also applies to the technical aspect, making composite materials a potential basis for components ranging in size from the very small to the very large.

One of the most important points is the structural capability of composite materials. This is illustrated by their use for airframe structures, race-car chassis, the hulls and structural bulkheads of boats and ships, robotics, and a range of commercial applications too wide to list.

That long list of applications is added to daily, which illustrates the

Probably one of the first major structural applications for modern composite materials was a Supermarine Spitfire fuselage, built during World War 2 from Gordon Aerolite. This material consisted of phenolic-resin-impregnated flax (linen) fibres. The component parts were held under pressure in a mould and cured at elevated temperature

From the early composite beginning in the Spitfire fuselage, progress and confidence in use have led to composites being utilized in almost all modern airliners, such as this European A320 Airbus.

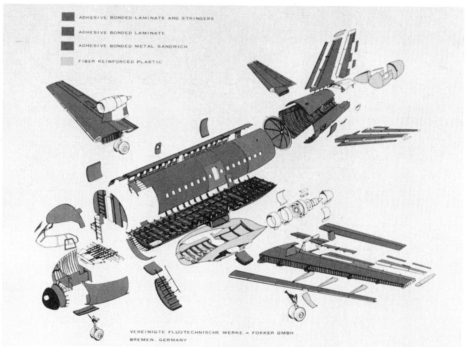

ADHESIVE BONDED LAMINATE AND STRINGERS

ADHESIVE BONDED LAMINATE

ADHESIVE BONDED METAL SANDWICH

FIBER REINFORCED PLASTIC

VEREINIGTE FLUGTECHNISCHE WERKE – FOKKER GMBH
BREMEN, GERMANY

This photograph shows the extent to which composites have been utilized by the aircraft industry

versatility of composite technology. Its many uses, ranging from the experimental Spitfire fuselage through the much later applications, such as advanced sports equipment, tennis rackets, golf clubs, etc, to advanced aerospace structures and race-car chassis, show the great advances that have been made during the first 35 years of modern composite development.

Several individuals and companies provided valuable assistance during the writing of this book, and I would particularly like to thank the following: Ciba-Geigy Plastics, Owen Corning Fiberglass (GB) Ltd, Vosper Thornycroft (UK) Ltd, E. Allman and Sons, Lola-Cars Ltd, Lola-Composites Ltd, Ivan Colby, Nigel Leaper and CFM Metalfax Ltd.

Keith Noakes NOVEMBER 1988

1 Adhesives

The vast number of differing adhesives—that is chemically and physically—and their many variants would yield sufficient information for a book on adhesives alone. However, as adhesives can form important parts in some composite structures, a range of adhesive systems that are most likely to be used in conjunction with modern composites will be outlined.

The choice of adhesive for the job in hand will depend on many factors, among them the adherends (that is the materials to be bonded), the available equipment, and the required performance from the bonded area in service.

Adhesives come in many physical forms and include brushable and sprayable liquids, which can also be curtain or roller coated. Curtain coating refers to a low-viscosity adhesive being poured to form a continuous curtain, through which the part to be bonded passes, usually on a moving conveyor; roller coating can be carried out by hand or by using automatic rollers and conveyors. Adhesives also come in paste forms that can be brushed into place or applied with a spreader or comb. The latter is usually a serrated or toothed spreader. The depth of serrations, or teeth, controls the wet thickness of the applied adhesive. This is a very useful method of application by hand.

The adhesives used in modern composite structures can be a mixture of a liquid and a dry, granular powder. The method of application consists of applying the liquid, followed by the granular component; the surplus is then shaken off. The amount of the granular compound that remains stuck to the liquid produces the correct ratio of the two parts; by varying the granular size, the ratio of the two parts can be altered.

Film and sheet-form adhesives are widely used in structural applications. They tend to be high-performance adhesives, and special equipment is required to utilize them, as will be described later. An obvious advantage is that the correct amount, or thickness, of adhesive can always be applied. Also, it can be cut accurately to size or shape, and it minimizes problems from the health and safety points of view, mainly due to the

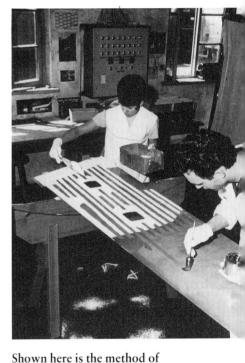

Shown here is the method of utilizing liquid-and-powder structural adhesive. This aircraft skin component is having the liquid part of the adhesive painted in the exact areas where stiffening members are to be bonded on. Another person is sprinkling the powder on to the liquid. Then the component is turned over and the excess powder shaken off. What remains stuck to the liquid produces the correct liquid-to-powder ratio

ABOVE   A completed aircraft component with bonded top-hat stringers is shown here being inspected prior to use

ABOVE RIGHT   This photograph shows clearly the use of elevated-temperature-curing adhesive to bond stiffening members in place

fact that most film adhesives are dry or solvent-free.

There are solid forms of adhesives that melt at elevated temperatures and then provide a bond when cooled. These types tend not to be used to any great extent in the areas covered by this book, but are useful due to the almost instant bond they provide. They can be used as a temporary fixing in assemblies which have loose components that require holding in place during assembly with the primary adhesive.

In addition to the many physical forms of adhesive, there are many types of curing reaction, and this is a major factor when selecting an adhesive system.

One important consideration is the pot life, or open time, of the adhesive. In general, these terms apply to liquid and paste forms of adhesive, and refer to the time that the adhesive remains in a usable state once opened or mixed. The user must consider this point in relation to component assembly time, to avoid a situation where the adhesive begins to go off before all of it has been applied or before the component has been assembled. Therefore, it is important to select the adhesive system that gives sufficient working time and that is suitable for the available equipment.

Adhesive cures can be actuated by various methods. Some are by evaporation, which can mean water or solvent loss; others employ a chemical reaction caused by the acid or other chemical catalysts and hardeners used in two-part adhesives. Water-activated adhesive systems are also widely used, as are thermo, or hot-set, systems.

With the hot-set type of cure, in some cases, the adhesive is applied as a liquid, which is dried, usually by solvent loss, before the final elevated-temperature cure takes place as a second stage. Elevated-temperature curing systems in film form are widely used, as previously described.

Adhesive types

The chemical bases for the most widely used adhesives include PVA, a water-based system popular for bonding wood, which is a single-part, cold-setting, air-activated adhesive. There are other water-based, wood-bonding adhesives, but as wood is not considered a major material for modern composites, it is not intended to go further on the subject, other than to say that resorcinal-based wood glues are used where extreme environmental conditions are expected.

Polyurethane adhesives in liquid form are used where large areas need bonding, their ease of application rendering them suitable for this application. In addition, they have the ability to bond a wide range of materials, including foam in rigid forms, metal, GRP, melamine and many others. Most polyurethane systems are cold- or warm-cured, the cure being activated by moisture. Therefore, the cure can be accelerated by the application of extra water by means of a spray. These types of adhesives, although giving good results in shear, tensile and peel on a wide range of materials, are not usually adopted in any of these modes when the highest structural performance is required.

In addition to being a good general-purpose system for large areas, polyurethane adhesives have, in most cases, good working-temperature resistance and environmental performance.

Acrylic adhesive systems do have some useful applications in the world of modern composites, but their limiting factors are the difficulty of application over large areas, a tendency to offer poor resistance to solvent and chemical attack, and their high cost. They are, however, very tough, which can be an important factor when choosing an adhesive.

Phenolic adhesives may be in liquid form, being cured by elevated temperatures in the region of 150°C; some liquid systems, however, are cured by acid catalyst. Phenolics may also be in film form, again elevated-temperature cured, or, as previously described, a liquid and powder combination.

In some forms, phenolics are good adhesives for bonding metal to metal, and also non-metallic materials to metallic ones. A renowned application is the bonding of car brake linings to their shoes. For many years phenolics have also been used in aircraft structures, although to much lesser extent in recent times.

In most cases, processing phenolic adhesive requires special equipment to produce the required elevated temperature and pressure during the cure. Pressure is very important, due to these types of systems producing water vapour and, therefore, internal pressure, which must be overcome to ensure a fully consolidated adhesive layer.

Phenolics are renowned for their extremely good environmental performance, but they have been replaced in recent years by other chemical

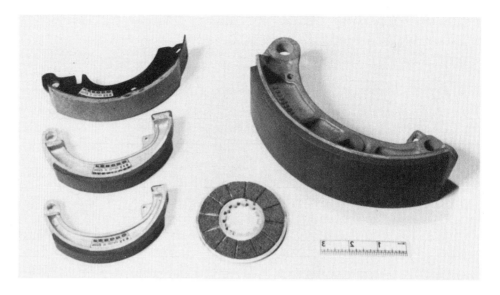

Adhesive performance can be so reliable that some types have been developed to bond vehicle brake linings to the shoes, replacing rivets. Samples are shown here; but this is a very special application, requiring very special knowledge and equipment

systems that can be easily modified to give the required specific performance.

Epoxy resin has probably been modified and supplied in more forms, and for more applications, than any other system.

Epoxy adhesives can be in liquid, paste or dry-film forms. They can also be cold-, warm- or hot-curing and, to add to their versatility, can be modified to meet a specific technical requirement. For example, they can be plasticized to give good peel performance, produced in a more brittle form to give high shear strength, or toughened to give high tensile strength and all-round high performance. Epoxy systems will also accept many additives to enhance other specific needs.

Apart from the availability of a wide range of epoxy forms, other advantages include great stability in the cured form, and resistance to a very wide range of chemical attack, although their resistance to exterior exposure and water is not considered as good as other chemical resin systems.

Epoxy adhesives only require contact pressure during their cure, that is sufficient pressure to ensure contact of the parts to be bonded. This applies to both cold and elevated-temperature cures. It means that, in many cases, bonding can be carried out without special equipment.

Overall stability, chemical resistance, etc are usually considered better in the cases of elevated-temperature cures, but this cannot be taken as a golden rule.

These notes are intended as a guide only to some possible adhesive systems, their chemical families and the main points regarding their uses, together with their advantages and disadvantages. There will be many other known adhesives and chemical types, such as the wide range of contact adhesives, the instant glues, and many more, but, although important in some cases, these do not fall into the area of modern composites covered by this book.

This book is intended as a basic guide to available adhesive systems and their use. However, as development continually produces advances in adhesive technology, and as there are many producers and many adhesive systems in each chemical category, it is possible that some points in this book may be contrary to the claims of some manufacturers. Consequently, users should select the correct form of the most suitable system for the job in hand, following the manufacturer's instructions regarding its use.

Selection and processing

For everyday make-and-mend use, there may be several adhesive types suitable for the job in hand. In addition, there may be several manufacturers supplying the selected type, and there can be differing performance and application claims from each manufacturer. So the choice is wide. The most important point with this type of bonding or repairing is to ensure that the chemical form is suitable for the materials to be bonded. Manufacturers' instructions usually explain the range of materials each adhesive will bond.

When it comes to production bonding, that is the bonding of larger areas, or continuous or repetitive bonding, there are many considerations to be taken into account. These include selecting adhesives to suit the materials to be bonded, especially if they are dissimilar; the equipment required to carry out the bonding, which should take into account the viability of the process; and, the most important consideration, the selection of an adhesive that meets the performance required from the finished component. This is where consideration has to be given to aspects such as hot strength, which should be in line with the working temperature of the finished component; this also applies to low-temperature use. Environmental and chemical resistance may also be important to the finished component.

This amazing advertisement for cold-curing, two-part epoxy adhesive shows a car bonded to a hoarding, with a second car on its roof

The environmental or performance requirement may dictate the adhesive type which, in turn, may enforce the use of special equipment. For example, to achieve high-temperature performance from an adhesive system normally requires the use of the hot-cured variety, although this is not a golden rule.

Where the adhesive is used in a structural application, other considerations apply, such as the ultimate strength requirement; and whether the bonded area will be loaded in shear, tension, peel, or more than one mode.

Structural adhesives are often produced by modification of a basic system to give variants that excel in one particular mode. For example, adhesives designed to give high peel strength will not perform to the maximum in shear. This is because the adhesive needs to be plasticized, or made flexible, to achieve good peel strength, yet it must be harder, or more brittle, to achieve high shear strength.

There will be many cases where the adhesive has to meet several or all the strength modes, in which case versions of the adhesive system will be modified to achieve an acceptable all-round performance.

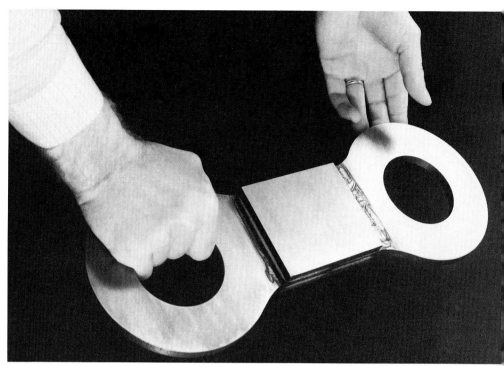

ABOVE   The performance of a lap-shear specimen (arrowed) is demonstrated in this photograph, which shows it supporting a 10-ton tanker

ABOVE RIGHT   An Araldite (two-part epoxy) double-lap shear specimen.

These variations enable the designer or user to select an adhesive for general, all-round performance or, where required, to achieve the ultimate strength in a particular mode.

In addition to ensuring good performance in shear, peel, etc, adhesive systems are also modified for other requirements. Elevated-temperature performance is one important area. Structural adhesive systems are now being widely used where a high percentage of the bond performance is retained at working temperatures in excess of 200°C. Adhesives developed for high-temperature use do not, as a rule, offer the maximum obtainable performance at ambient temperature. These points must be considered when the bonded component is being designed; that is the bond area will be arrived at by taking into account the strength required from the component and the capability of the adhesive at the component's working temperature.

Sub-zero-temperature performance may also be an important criterion in the case of components stressed in shear, and particularly when epoxy resins are being used. The strength can actually improve. This is due to the low-temperature effect causing the adhesive to become harder, which is an advantage in the case of shear strength, and can also be useful in some tensile applications. However, where peel strength is concerned, in almost all cases, this shows a drop in performance. The flexibility required for good peel strength is reduced at very low temperatures.

Chemical resistance may also be built in. Again, epoxy resins have a good, natural chemical resistance, which can be modified to meet specific needs, but one enemy of resin systems is water, particularly if the component spends some time dry and some wet. This problem is magnified if changing temperatures are also involved. Epoxy-based adhesives can be modified to give a good performance under these conditions, due to their other excellent qualities, which include ease of processing. Phenolic-resin-based adhesives have better natural resistance to water and environmental exposure but, as previously stated, are more difficult to process.

Although some cold-set adhesive systems have reasonably good all-round chemical and environmental resistance, to achieve the ultimate possible performance in these areas, adhesives of any chemical type will usually have to be of the elevated-temperature-curing variety.

Major considerations are the application method and time required. For example, when two-part liquid or paste-type adhesives are being considered, their pot life is important, that is the time they remain usable after the two parts have been mixed. This pot life should not be less than the time needed to assemble a complex component or to cover a large area. Pot life should also be borne in mind from the point of view of equipment, where time must be allowed to clean down before the adhesive gels off.

Liquid and paste adhesives can be applied by several methods. They can be brushed on, or sprayed or roller coated, either automatically or by hand.

Serious consideration should be given to the thickness of the applied coating. When using film adhesives this factor is controlled automatically by the thickness of the film supplied. In some cases, the thickness may not be an important or necessary consideration, but in others it may be critical.

Adhesive suppliers will specify the optimum thickness for any particular adhesive to ensure the ultimate performance from that particular system; even coating may, or may not, be important. Roller coating or spraying will give a good, even application, but applying paste-type adhesives by combing is an excellent method of application to achieve a controlled coating thickness. After the adhesive has been applied to the surface, it is spread by pulling a comb across the surface.

Combs usually take the form of saw-edged implements. The pitch and depth of the teeth provide very accurate control of the wet thickness of adhesive. This type of application is particularly suitable for applying adhesive over larger areas, as it is important to maintain an even thickness. Uneven applications can require immense pressure to prevent the formation of thick adhesive layers, which can be detrimental to the potential strength of the bond.

During the selection of the adhesive, another aspect to be considered is the required curing cycle. This, as mentioned previously, will depend on the adhesive type and the available equipment; that is, where elevated-temperature curing is to be carried out, a heated press or some other method of heating, such as an autoclave or oven, will be required.

In the main, a press will be used for flat, or almost flat, components. It usually consists of steel platens heated by electricity or steam; both methods of heating have advantages. Electrical heating will give a higher temperature than is possible with steam; but platens drilled for steam

Shown here is a steam-heated platen press used to make sandwich panels or laminates

Vacuum tables or presses come in many forms. Shown here is a wooden version with metal top face, but purpose-built commercial versions are available

Stiffening components, such as bars, ribs or top-hat stringers, can be located during bonding by special tooling or rivets. The adhesive cure takes place in a press or in an oven, under vacuum or under pressure in an autoclave. This photograph shows such a component with straddle bars in place, which apply the pressure to the required area

heating utilize the steamways for the passage of cooling water and, therefore, effect a much faster cooling of the bonded component. This cooling can be an asset with components utilizing dissimilar materials, or some metallic components, where bowing or distortion could be a problem resulting from hot adhesive cures.

Although presses are used primarily for making flat components, where two-part tools or moulds of fairly shallow shape are to be used, and are of a suitable material to withstand the temperature and the pressure, the press is a suitable method for effecting the adhesive cure.

Adhesives cured under positive pressure and at elevated temperature can be used in two-part jigs or tools, either metallic or high-performance resin, pressure being applied by clamp bolts or turn-screws. It is normal to use high-pressure springs in conjunction with the clamping device, which gives follow-up pressure during the cure. This not only caters for adhesive systems that are dependent on pressure during the cure, but also ensures correct mating of the component parts. The jig or tool is then raised and held at the required cure temperature in some form of oven.

Where the component parts to be bonded are of complex or irregular shape, making the use of matched tools difficult, the adhesive and its method of application can be the same as before, but the bonding pressure can be applied by the use of vacuum. The method is to assemble component parts into the jig, mould or tool, followed by any mould top halves, or pressure plates. This assembly is then covered with a vacuum blanket, which can consist of a purpose-made, silicone-rubber sheet, either tailored from stock flat material, or moulded to shape if this is complex. The vacuum blanket, or cover, may incorporate some form of frame around the periphery, which serves as the retainer for some form of clamp to hold and seal the blanket to the lower part, or bed, of the tool or mould.

Air is removed through a vacuum take-off in the blanket or peripheral frame, using a vacuum pump. The resultant vacuum supplies the pressure to hold the components being bonded in place and together. Under full vacuum, the pressure applied to the assembly is one atmosphere (14.69 psi). The assembly is allowed to stand, in the case of cold-set adhesives, or is placed in an oven for elevated-temperature cures.

When an elevated-temperature cure is being used, it is advisable to place a thermocouple connection in, or close to, the glue line to register the temperature at that point. This will ensure that the temperature is kept to the supplier's recommendation, achieving the optimum performance from the adhesive system being used. One common fault when using elevated-temperature-curing adhesives is to time the cure from when the oven reaches the required temperature, without allowing the tooling to heat up; and with heavy tools or moulds this can take a long time.

The thermocouple is usually a fine wire attached to a sensitive temperature-recording instrument, the wire being long enough to be used in large ovens or autoclaves. This part of the operation is important on individual tooling. In the case of a press, the platen temperature is automatically recorded on the press itself.

Although this level of pressure is sufficient for many applications, in some cases, much higher pressure is required to ensure the mating of the component parts. The adhesive itself can demand higher pressure, as is the case with some phenolic versions, although in general use, phenolic adhesives are not very common outside the aircraft industry.

One major consideration when any adhesive bonding is to be designed into a component, or for any straightforward, simple joining of materials, is the pre-treatment, or surface preparation, of the parts to be joined; these are usually referred to as the adherends.

There are several reasons why it is necessary to carry out some form of preparation to the surface to be bonded. In the case of metal, it is to remove any layer of oxide on the surface. On non-ferrous metals, aluminium and alloys, the oxide layer is usually of low tensile strength, or is softer than the base material. This causes a weak interface at the bonded joint. In the case of various steels, millscale, or the hardened surface caused by rolling, can also cause problems. One important aspect of bonding metallic components is that without any pre-treatment, or with sub-standard surface preparation, not only is the ultimate strength of the bonded joint likely to be affected, but the environmental performance will also be impaired.

The most widely-used method of pre-treatment for aluminium and aluminium alloys is acid etching, in most cases to a recognized specification; for example, DTD 915B11, which is a British specification for a chromic/sulphuric solution. This solution can be used at room temperature, but by heating the solution to 64°C, the time required to effect the pre-treatment is cut from many hours to 30 minutes. After being acid etched, the part must be washed thoroughly in running water to remove all traces of acid. This is important, as are standard handling precautions with these types of chemicals.

With some metals, magnesium for instance, different acid solutions are necessary, together with a desmuting solution. However, due to the difficult and inconsistent results often achieved on these metals, mechanical pre-treatment is often used as an alternative.

Acid pre-treatment can be carried out on stainless steels, but each type of stainless steel requires a different acid solution and desmuting solution. Therefore, if acid-etching pre-treatment is essential, it is important that the correct formulation for the type of steel being used is discussed with the suppliers. Again, in most cases, the pre-treatment for this range of steels will be by mechanical means.

It is also possible for normal steels, including mild, to be pre-treated by the use of phosphate solutions where the surfaces are to be painted or bonded. When this form of pre-treatment is used, excellent bond strengths can result. However, the chemical balance of the solution can change without warning, producing a surface that, although the same visually, provides poor bond quality. So where bond strength is critical, or where large numbers of components are to be bonded, normal steels are best pre-treated mechanically.

Mechanical pre-treatment can take the form of abrasion by hand or by machine, that is with abrasive cloth or paper, or some of the many forms of grinding wheels and discs. Although better than no pre-treatment at all and, in some cases capable of producing good bond quality, this form of mechanical pre-treatment is not the most consistent, nor is it likely to produce the ultimate performance from the adhesive being used. These latter points, however, do not exclude this form of pre-treatment, as the performance capability of the adhesive system may be far in excess of the performance requirement from the bonded component; or there may be no alternative.

By far the most reliable and widely-used method of achieving the ultimate performance when bonding steels is by grit blasting. This can be carried out with a hand-operated or automatic machine, the nozzle of which delivers a jet of abrasive grit under pressure, usually from compressed air. The pressure and the abrasive qualities of the grit used will determine the amount of surface material removed by this method.

Abrasives for blasting can be glass beads, steel or iron shot, or alumina grit. All can be purchased in many grades, ranging from almost powder to quite large particle size; the type and size are selected to suit the job in hand—very small particles and low pressure for thin or delicate components, and large particles for heavier or stronger parts.

It is important to use the right type of abrasive; for example, glass

Another use for modern adhesives is shown here. They are being used in a car factory to bond body panels together

beads would not be suitable for the pre-treatment of heavy steel components. Soft, common steel shot, although suitable for paint treatment, is not ideal for the pre-treatment of parts to be bonded. This is due to the soft nature of the shot, which tends to disturb the surface being blasted, but does not remove the surface layer completely. It can also deposit some of the soft steel on the blasted surface. This is bad for bonding, as the deposit can be pulled off, producing a sub-standard bond.

Where metal grit is to be used, chilled cast-iron is preferable. This is angular in shape and of brittle nature, which causes the grit to break up in use, rather than wearing away, which means it retains its angular shape and cutting power much longer.

One important point regarding the use of iron shot is that it should never be used on aluminium or aluminium alloys. Although, in the short term, it will produce good bond quality, it can leave microscopic particles of iron embedded in the aluminium. Under certain circumstances, this can lead to an electrolitic reaction between the dissimilar metals, affecting the long-term strength of the bonded joint.

To eliminate the problems of incompatibility and have one abrasive suitable for pre-treating any metal, aluminium-oxide grit should be used. This retains its cutting shape as it breaks up in use, and is also supplied in various grit sizes, which can be selected to suit the job in hand, remembering that very large grit does not necessarily mean a better bond.

Whatever type of grit is used, if it is too small it may not have sufficient abrasive power; large grit on small components does not produce the best results either. The manufacturers of the adhesive will usually advise on the best grit type and size to suit both the adhesive and the parts or materials it is to bond.

Pre-treatment can be as important when bonding non-metallic materials as it is when bonding metals. However, the method used is not as critical as it is with metallic objects. In many cases, with GRP and other plastic materials, abrasion is a suitable pre-treatment method, as the aim is to remove any contaminated surface material, including release agents, and to present a roughened surface.

Some components in GRP, or other plastic materials, that are purpose-made to be bonded can have pre-treatment built-in by the use of a peel ply. This consists of a fine mesh material, usually nylon, which is moulded into the surface when the component is made. When the part is ready for bonding, prior to the application of the adhesive, the peel ply is stripped off. As it is peeled away, the resin that penetrated the weave of the material is pulled off, resulting in an even, rough, uncontaminated surface.

Grit blasting can be used on some hard resin surfaces, but it is imperative to use alumina grit.

The pre-treatment method for any surface or material will be recommended by the suppliers of the selected adhesive, but it is important to ensure that both the adhesive and the pre-treatment will meet the performance requirement of the finished component.

2 Laminating by wet lay-up

The term wet lay-up applies to the use of a liquid matrix resin in conjunction with synthetic fibres, or some other carrier material, to produce a laminate in some form. Wet lay-up usually implies that the laminating is carried out by hand. This method requires the minimum of equipment, and when cold-curing resin systems are used, the tooling can be comparatively simple and cheap.

With reasonable care, almost anyone can produce good laminated components by the wet lay-up process. Therefore, it is suitable for the average enthusiast wishing to utilize composites for some applications. The same basic method can also be used to manufacture high-performance components, or those that are too complex to produce by other methods.

This photograph shows the basic materials used to manufacture components by the wet lay-up method

The ultimate performance of components or parts made by the wet lay-up method is controlled, to a great degree, by the materials used. This applies to both the carrier fibre and the matrix-resin system. When selecting the materials, there are several points to consider; the structural requirement (if applicable), the component weight, environmental or working performance and, in many cases, the cost.

The most widely-used fibre types are carbon, Kevlar and glass. There are other, less widely-used types, such as boron fibre and Nomex.

In the case of carbon and glass, there are differing forms of actual fibre. Carbon, for instance, comes in high-strength versions and high-modulus types. There are many types of glass fibre, but there are two main forms used in composite structures. 'E' glass is the most widely used and forms the basis of most reinforcement fabrics used in laminating. 'R' glass is designed to give very high-modulus fibres, and is used in special high-performance laminates. These high-modulus glass fibres are much more expensive and less widely available.

The matrix-resin system selected must be capable of ensuring that the performance of the selected fibre is fully utilized, so that the design requirement is achieved. Selection must be based on several considerations: the performance requirement of the finished component, the equipment and expertise available to process the product, and commercial viability.

Matrix-resin systems used for laminating by the wet lay-up method fall into four main chemical groups: polyesters, vynlesters, epoxies and phenolics.

Polyester resins

There are many forms of polyester resin, some having higher-temperature performance, others plasticized, quick or slow curing systems. They are by far the most widely used in the manufacture of components by the wet lay-up method. This is due to two very important points: cost and simplicity. Polyester resins are not only cheaper in comparison to other chemical systems but, in general, they are also more tolerant of misuse and working environment.

Common uses for polyester-reinforced glass include automotive bodywork, canoes, pool liners, building panels, leisure equipment, furniture and shipbuilding. In fact, they can be found in almost any area where cheap moulded shapes are required.

The simplicity of polyester-resin systems is extended by the fact that very similar techniques are needed to make the tooling or moulds as the items to be moulded.

Vynlesters

These resin systems are becoming widely used, both for mould making and for laminated components. Like polyesters, they are comparatively simple to use, but vynlesters have two major advantages. One is that they produce a tougher laminate, which for mould making, in particular, is a great advantage. The other is that, in most cases, they also have much better high-temperature performance.

Vynlesters can be used for mould making or component lamination and totally cured at room temperature, but an added bonus is that, if the equipment is available (that is a suitable oven) or for technical reasons elevated-temperature performance is required, then the room-temperature-cured mould or component can be post-cured to achieve this elevated-temperature performance.

The post-cure consists of subjecting the mould or component to the required temperature, usually in the region of 140–150°C, for a specified period of time. These details will be noted on the manufacturer's data sheet for the selected resin system.

This post-cure capability makes moulds made with vynlesters suitable for use with elevated-temperature-curing pre-pregs, using a cure temperature up to approximately 125°C. For higher temperature cures, an epoxy mould will have to be considered.

Both vynlesters and polyesters work well as matrix-resin systems on glass-fibre carriers, whereas most available carbon fibres are treated to be epoxy-resin compatible. Vynlesters used on carbon fibre make laminating difficult, as they tend to drain away from the carbon surface.

It is unlikely, however, that any project would require the expense of carbon fibre as a carrier, when compared to the relatively low cost of polyester or vynlester resin systems. Performance-wise, carbon would not be justified either, unless the ultimate possible matrix-resin performance was selected.

Vynlester-resin systems now fill an important slot, cost-wise and performance-wise, between polyesters and epoxies.

Epoxy resins

Despite their greater cost, epoxy resins are now becoming more widely used, and this is due to greater available performance. This increase in performance can include greater stiffness for the same weight; higher working-temperature performance; and, very important in some cases, much greater stability. The last refers to the mechanical performance after manufacture being maintained over extended periods of time, unlike polyesters, which tend to soften with age, leading to distortion and fatigue cracking or stress relieving.

Epoxy-resin systems themselves can be modified by the manufacturer to give the desired mechanical or chemical performance and, often these performance requirements can be improved by the use of elevated-temperature curing, which takes place while the component is in the mould; in some cases, a post-cure can be used to improve a material's performance. This is achieved by reheating the component after removal from the mould, time and temperature being dependent on the resin system and the requirement. This, as with all other curing data, will be on the supplier's data sheet.

One obvious advantage of the post-cure technique is that while this operation is being carried out, the mould is available for manufacturing another component.

Although epoxy-based components can be manufactured in polyester moulds, in most cases, epoxy will be used for the matrix resin of the tooling or mould.

The added expense of using epoxy resins for the tooling can be justified in several ways. The ability to modify epoxy and to post-cure can result in greater mould stability from the dimensional point of view. The post-cure capability can have a great effect on the elevated-temperature performance of the mould, thus giving the added advantage of allowing elevated-temperature cures in this type of mould. Elevated-temperature cures can also be carried out in polyester moulds, but mould life, when used under elevated-temperature cure conditions, is usually much longer in the case of epoxy moulds.

Phenolics

Phenolic-resin systems are employed in some specialized component manufacture, but are seldom used as a tooling or mould matrix resin.

Phenolic resins, in many forms, have very good fire-retardant properties and, used in conjunction with selected fibres, lend themselves to the manufacture of moulded components or surfaces to meet fire-resistant standards. Phenolics also have the advantage that, should the temperature reach a high enough level to char or burn the laminate, less smoke is given off than with other resin systems; also very important is the fact that any gases produced as a result of charring or burning are much less toxic than from other resin systems.

Like other chemical resins, phenolics can be modified to enhance specific qualities. These special qualities make phenolics much more suitable than other well-known resin systems as matrix resins for laminating and for producing facing skins for sandwich panels intended for use in areas of high temperature, or in areas were flame-spread and fire-retardant regulations apply. Examples of the latter are interior panelling in ships or other personnel-carrying vehicles, building interiors, etc.

Phenolics used as matrix resins do not have as good mechanical properties as some other systems. Their structural performance, such as laminate or sandwich-panel stiffness, would be less for panels of the same dimensions; when phenolics are used for the outer skins of a sandwich panel, the bond to the sandwich core material is generally lower in peel strength. Phenolics also tend to be brittle.

Another important area of high performance, in addition to the fire-retardant properties of phenolic resins, is their resistance to chemical and atmospheric exposure.

In situations where the special qualities of phenolics are needed, but they would not normally meet the mechanical or structural requirements, in some cases, they can be used in conjunction with epoxy-resin systems to enhance the required properties.

An example of the use of combined resin systems is where the resin, with some form of fibre, is to form the facing skins of a sandwich panel requiring the fire-retardant properties of phenolics, but a structural performance in excess of the phenolic's capability. In this case, epoxy-resinated fibres would be used next to the core material. This would give the required core-to-skin peel strength and show an improved panel stiffness.

There are many considerations to be taken into account when a panel or component is being designed around specific performance requirements. In some cases, where weight is not a consideration, the use of additional laminate layers may be sufficient, or the level of performance might fall within the capability of the phenolic-resin system being used.

Phenolic-resin systems have been manufactured for many years in many forms, but they are not as widely used as other well-known chemical systems, and there are several reasons for this. Among these are the very special, but limited, performance criteria, and the more complicated handling and processing requirements.

In general, phenolics have a more complicated curing process, particularly when cold-curing is required. Theoretically, phenolics can be cold-cured by acid activation, but to achieve the special performance capability, in most cases, the component must be subjected to post-cure. This means removing the component from the mould after its room-temperature cure when it is stable enough to be self-supporting. It is then oven-cured at elevated temperature.

Phenolics also produce water during the cure and, therefore, generate internal pressure. In some cases, where very thick laminates are being made, or skins being bonded on to honeycomb core materials, 'breathing' may be necessary. This means that the bonding pressure is released then reapplied immediately, allowing the internal pressure to be released. This problem of internal pressure does not generally apply to wet lay-up phenolics, as these are not, as yet, very widely used. In the cases where they are used, it is rare for them to be hot-cured under pressure. These points become much more important with the use of phenolic pre-pregs as described later.

Phenolics cannot be self-coloured to any practical standard, as the colour tends to darken during curing or with age. This colour change is far more pronounced in the case of elevated-temperature curing. Therefore, it is usual for phenolic-based components requiring a decorative finish to have that finish applied as a final process.

Making moulds

To produce a component by the wet-lay-up method, whatever the matrix resin used, it is essential to use a mould. This can be male or female, that is the part can be made on the mould (male) or in the mould (female).

The form of mould used is decided by two main points: the first is the shape of the component, coupled with ease of manufacture; the second is surface finish. The surface formed against the mould will be as good as the mould surface.

A buck, or pattern, will be required to produce the mould, and there are various methods and materials that can be used in its construction. Again, size and shape will play major roles in the selection of both method and material. For example, a small pattern would usually be solid, and could be of wood, plaster, foam, and various fillers. With larger bucks, or patterns, a hollow construction is used and can be based on a plywood box-like former, the approximate size and shape of the component. This is covered with plaster, resin-based filler, or some material that can be carved or sanded to the required shape and finish.

The process is the same for both male and female mould patterns, and there are occasions when the pattern or mould, or both, have to be made in more than one piece, due to the component's shape preventing it from being moulded in a one-piece mould. Sometimes matched tooling is required. This is used when both inner and outer surfaces of the component are moulded. To achieve this, two patterns are required for one mould; one to produce the female mould face, and one to produce the male face or surface.

An early stage in the manufacture of a wood-and-filler buck, or pattern

Applying a resin coat to the buck, or pattern, so that it can be polished to give the mould a smooth surface

A widely used material for patterns is painted wood. An example is shown here

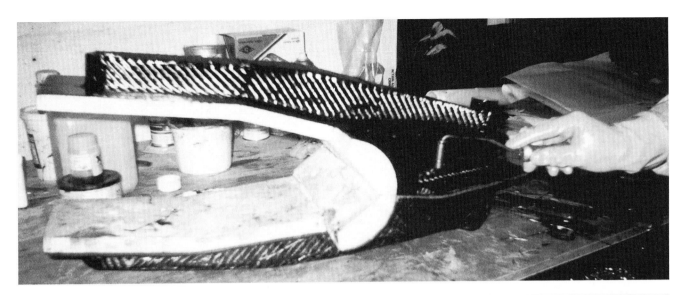

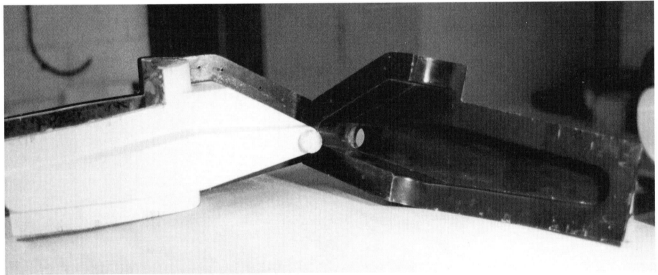

Due to the complication and inherent cost of using matched moulds, this method would only be adopted where the component thickness was a very critical requirement, or the inner and outer component surfaces are different.

There is a slightly cheaper method of making matching moulds, which can be used when component thickness is important, but not ultra critical. This begins with the manufacture of a male or female mould, into which is formed a sheet of some thermo-softening material, such as a plastic or foam, of the same thickness as that required for the finished component. In some cases, the thermo-softening material is formed into the mould with the use of vacuum.

The plastic or foam material is trimmed to the contours of the required component and left in place while a second mould is cast or laminated on to it. When set, or cured, this second mould is removed, followed by removal of the thermo-softening material. The result is one mould that

TOP A mould being made by the wet lay-up method, using epoxy resin and carbon fibre. The method would be similar for other mould materials.

ABOVE Removing a two-part carbon fibre mould from the pattern

fits inside the other, leaving a cavity between the two that represents the dimensions of the required component.

The component is then cast or laminated into the cavity, and the two moulds are compressed together. The result is a finished component with both inner and outer surfaces of mould-quality finish, as well as having a more constant overall thickness.

Having produced the pattern to allow moulds to be taken off that suit both mould and component construction, materials must be selected to meet the curing requirements of the laminating resin to be used in the mould. Where wet lay-up laminating is to be employed, in most cases, the cure will be at room temperature, which means that almost any tooling resin can be used. However, if the cure is to be at elevated temperature, and/or the mould will be required to produce very large numbers of components, then much more effort must be put into the selection of a suitable tooling resin.

If the mould is to be of a solid cast type, which can be used when the pattern is of a shallow or flat configuration, the resin system should be designed for this specific purpose.

Epoxy-resin systems are the most widely used for cast moulds, and there are several reasons for this, including the fact that they can be modified to overcome exothermic problems. In other words, when used in bulk, as in a cast mould, the heat generated by the reactive curing process can be controlled. There are degrees of exotherm, ranging from temperatures that cause severe internal bubbling of the resin, which destroys the mould, to temperature rises high enough to cause a resin fire.

Another very important reason for the choice of epoxy resin for cast moulds is that they can be modified by the supplier to minimize shrinkage. Epoxy resins can also be very stable in the fully-cured state, which means that dimensional stability can be optimized and maintained over extended periods of mould life.

Whatever the chosen chemical resin system, the basic method of mould construction will be similar.

Because of the wide range of resin systems, and the many variants of each system, compounded by the many suppliers and their own particular variants, it is not intended to describe the use of any specific make of resin system.

The choice of resin system will be based on technical performance, cost or simplicity of use. Having chosen one to meet the requirements for a cast mould, the first stage is to prepare the pattern prior to casting. If the pattern is of wood or a plaster-type material, surface sealing will be necessary. This consists of coating the pattern's surface with one of the many available sealers. Then the sealed surface is polished to leave a smooth, non-porous finish. This type of finish is essential to ensure the release of the mould from the pattern and, in turn, the mould requires the same extra-smooth finish for the release of the laminated component, and to provide a good component finish.

At this point, the pattern will have been prepared fully and, if necessary, will include split lines, that is where the mould is made in sections. This may be to assist removal of the finished component from the mould or, in some cases, be essential due to the shape of the component.

Split lines are achieved by adding a temporary divider of some sort—plastic sheet, thin plywood etc—to the mould. One section of the mould is formed up to the divider. When the section of mould has cured, the divider is removed and the next section, or remainder of the mould, is formed. The mould sections are held together by some mechanical means, such as bolts or clamps, while the component is being laminated. Split lines are not as widely used on solid cast moulds as they are on the larger laminated moulds.

The final stage before producing the mould is to apply a release agent to the pattern. The type of release agent used will depend on many things—the chemical composition of the resin system; whether an elevated-temperature cure will be involved; and, in some cases, personal choice.

There are many forms of release agent: wax, which is widely used on cold-set systems; silicone liquids; and many proprietary non-silicone liquid systems. PVA emulsions are also used, some of them being suitable for high-temperature use on metallic moulds. The choice is greatly extended by the fact that there are also many manufacturers. If little or no knowledge of these materials prevails, the simple answer is to accept the recommendations of the supplier or manufacturer of the chosen resin system.

The method of release-agent application is also open to choice, and may be by cloth pad, brush or spray; some release agents are supplied in ready-to-use aerosol cans. Once again, the release-agent supplier will recommend a suitable application method to suit the prevailing conditions or performance requirement.

When ready for the casting process, the pattern will be placed in a suitable tray or shallow box. This is to retain the liquid casting resin and to control the resin depth or mould thickness. In most cases where cast moulds are used, epoxy resin is utilized for the reasons described previously.

Whatever the type of resin system, it will normally utilize a catalyst or hardener, which will have to be added to the resin at the manufacturer's specified mixing ratio. In the case of casting resin, the ratio is extremely important to prevent exotherm problems. However, mixing ratios should be taken seriously with all types of resin mix. This ensures that the casting or lamination reaches a fully-cured state.

In most cases, the mixing ratio can be measured by weight or volume. If the ratio is to be arrived at by weight, it is advisable to use a very accurate balance or set of scales. Normally, electronic laboratory-type balances are used, especially if the catalyst is of a very reactive type which needs adding in a very small proportion. Measuring portions by volume can be as effective, but it is always difficult to allow for what is retained on the surface of the measuring vessels.

A gel coat being applied by hand. This method would apply to both mould and component

RIGHT   The double-stage method of mould making. The component second from the left is the first pattern, from which the first female mould is taken (shown on the right of the pattern). This is made using conventional two-part, cold-curing resins with gel coat. Note the egg-boxed honeycomb sandwich support frames. Into this mould is laminated a component using two-part epoxy resin that can be post-cured at elevated temperature; in this case, the fibre is carbon.

Mixing instructions will be given in the supplier's data but, in almost all cases, hand stirring is acceptable. Mechanical mixing is more desirable for large-volume mixes, and in some rare cases where the mixing process should be long and controlled.

The resin system can often be modified to enhance a specific performance requirement. For example, fillers can be added to improve temperature resistance. Aluminium powder is used for this purpose, as is ceramic powder. Other fillers can be added to improve mould hardness and toughness. Among these are slate powders and ground mineral products. Again, advice from the resin supplier will ensure that both the performance is met and the filler is compatible with the chosen resin system.

It is general practice in mould manufacture to use a gel coat, which is a layer of resin applied to the pattern and cured, or part-cured, prior to pouring the main bulk of the resin.

In some cases, the gel coat is a special modified version of the mould resin supplied by the manufacturer. The aim is to get a dense, void-free surface next to the pattern. If supplied as a gel coat, the resin will usually be lower in viscosity, that is thinner, which ensures that the surface is completely wetted out. Any filler present will have a very small particle size to assist a smooth surface. Where the normal resin is to be used as a gel coat, to achieve a good mould surface finish, it should also be applied as a thin coat without a filler, assuming fillers are being used.

When the gel coat has cured or, in some cases, part-cured, the remainder of the required resin is mixed and poured over the gel-coated pattern to a level that gives the required mould depth or thickness.

It is common practice to put additional filler material into the back-up resin. One simple filler is clean sand. This gives the mould extra toughness, helps to reduce dimensional changes of the cured mould, reduces the risk of exotherm, and cuts costs by reducing the resin quantity required to fill a given space.

Until experience has been gained, it is always important to follow the manufacturer's instructions or recommendations. As the permutation of resin types, manufacturers, manufacturers' modifications, fillers and additives is almost endless, and there are constant changes and developments, it is impossible to chronical every system or method.

Once the cast mould is fully cured, it can be separated from the pattern. If the mould has been made in sections, removal will be easy. If it is a single casting, it will usually be tough enough to withstand moderate tapping, and the shock waves caused by the tapping should be sufficient to remove the pattern from the mould. In some cases, where the pattern is made from easily-damaged materials, such as plaster or some type of foam, it is quicker to simply cut the pattern into sections to remove it.

The method of mould release should be given some consideration, and in particular whether it is important for the pattern to be reusable or not, as this will effect the choice of material from which it is made.

In certain circumstances, where the final component is to be made in large numbers and the moulds may need frequent replacement, it may be worth considering making the first mould from the pattern using a flexible mould material, such as silicone rubber. This material is available in forms designed for this type of application.

The rubber mould thickness should be arranged to give sufficient stability so that a cheap pattern material, such as plaster of Paris or similar, can be cast into it; the mould's flexibility allows the pattern to be removed easily. The resultant pattern is then sealed and used to make the resin mould. With this method, the pattern can be remade as many times as required, very simply and cheaply, once the initial high cost of mould material and the extra time involved has been absorbed.

Silicone rubbers for mould making come in various forms, but are usually two-part mixtures that cure at room temperature. Other proprietary flexible mould-making materials are also available. In most cases, advice on a system suitable for the project in hand can be obtained from the resin suppliers or the many firms factoring composite supplies.

Subject to normal preparation, the solid cast mould is now ready for use.

The more common method of mould making is by lamination. From a basic technique, a wide range of differing qualities can be achieved, depending on the type of resin system and carrier chosen. The carrier can be of the fibre type and form and will be resin impregnated to make the mould.

This component is post-cured out of the first mould, which has limited temperature performance. The male component is then used to make the final female mould. As the post-cure applied to the pattern raises its temperature resistance, the final mould can be made with pre-preg, or high-temperature-curing tooling resin. The resultant mould, shown on the extreme left, can then be used to produce components like the aircraft part being held in this photograph, in an oven or autoclave under high pressure and at elevated temperature. Carbon fibre is used for the second pattern and final mould because of its low coefficient of expansion, which enables much closer dimensional tolerances to be held

The quality of the mould depends on whether its construction is based on cost or technical performance. The latter can mean a mould that requires extremely accurate dimensional stability, a similar coefficient of expansion to the component being made in the mould, or the ability to withstand elevated temperatures.

In many cases, the performance requirement from the mould determines, to a great extent, the choice of resin system used. For example, for very high-temperature use, epoxy would be used in preference to polyester, although there are polyester systems capable of withstanding elevated-temperature cures. The actual temperature and duration at high temperature are the critical points. Where elevated temperature is to be used, the dimensions of the finished component are not critical, and only one or two components are needed, it is possible to utilize polyester to reduce costs, but mould life will be short. Where the life needs to be long, or the mould capable of many off-takes, coupled with the use of elevated temperatures, then epoxy resin would be more suitable. In cases where carbon fibre is to be used as the carrier, epoxy would also be the ideal matrix-resin system.

Epoxy-resin systems are in the region of three or four times the cost of polyester resins, but polyesters, in general, are simpler to use. They tend to be less sensitive to mixing ratio, although every effort should be made to get this right. When the ratio and the mixing method is carried out to the instructions, in many cases, the mixed polyester can be applied in larger quantities than is normal with epoxy systems. Often polyesters cure faster than epoxies and, therefore, can reduce the overall mould-making time, especially if the particular mould is to have a thick section which would require several laminated layers, requiring cures or part cures between layers.

Whatever resin system is selected, the basic laminating process will be similar.

Again, a gel coat is an important part of the process; in fact, with wet laminating moulds, where fibre carriers are to be used, it is essential. This is to ensure that the mould surface is resin only, that is the surface layer must be free of fibres, ensuring that the mould surface remains smooth, even if it has to be dressed or polished during its usable life.

With both polyester and epoxy wet laminating resins, normally it is practical to use the same resin as is to be used for the main laminating job. Sometimes it is advisable to add a small quantity of some form of inert filler; the resin supplier will advise on and supply this. The only purpose of the filler is to raise the viscosity of, or thicken, the resin to help prevent it from running off the pattern or forming puddles if the pattern is a female form.

With many laminating resins the suppliers offer specially-prepared gel coats, which contain any necessary filler and wetting agents. In some cases, the resin used for the gel coat will be denser, or harder, to give the mould surface better wear properties.

Special gel coats are not exclusive to epoxy resins, but the ease with which manufacturers can modify them to meet special needs is the reason why there is a much wider choice available to meet most specific needs. This also applies to the range of laminating resins.

Before laminating can begin, a reasonable estimate of the amount of resin required must be made. The amount of resin and fibre used for any specific application will depend on several factors: the resin and fibre types, the intended ratio of resin to fibre and, very important, the skill or expertise of the laminator.

First of all, the thickness of the finished laminate should be decided, although this is not a critical dimension, provided the mould has a wall thickness sufficient to prevent it going out of shape during use. The way in which this is prevented will be described later. The mould's wall thickness will depend, to some degree, on its overall size, but this is not a significant factor. It means, however, that the wall thickness of very large moulds, such as those for a boat, would usually be much greater than that of a mould for a small component.

Having decided on the approximate thickness of your laminated mould, you should also decide on what fibre carrier is to be used. As an approximate guide, measure the total thickness of the intended number of fibre layers, and then assume that the resin needed to wet out this quantity of fibre would have a cured thickness approximately equal to that of the fibre layers. Using this resin thickness and the approximate area or size of the mould, you can simply calculate the required volume of the resin. This will assist in determining the cost of the mould, or the amount of resin to purchase.

One important point, is that, whatever the thickness of the mould wall, you do not have to mix all the resin at once.

In fact, in the case of large or thick moulds, it is important not to mix all the resin in one batch, for two reasons. Large volumes of mixed resin often have a much shorter pot life, that is the time that the resin remains usable after mixing, than small quantities; and in the case of a very large or complicated mould, it may not be possible to laminate up to full thickness within the pot life of the mixed resin.

Where the mould has a very thick wall, it will have to be part laminated, allowed to cure, or part-cure, before adding more laminations until the required thickness has been achieved. This gradual building up to thickness serves to prevent the problem of an exotherm occurring in the laminate, which would cause serious problems and could destroy the mould.

As stated, there are no set rules for assessing how thick a mould should be. A complex mould will gain considerable stiffness from its shape, but a large area with very little change of shape will need to be thicker. Laminated moulds can be as thin as 2 or 3 mm for very small moulds, but between 5 and 10 mm covers the widest range of moulds. Extremely large moulds for large boats or ship hulls will, of course, be much thicker.

The resin system may have considerable effect on the mould thickness. For example, epoxy-resin-based moulds can generally be thinner than polyester-based versions, due to the additional stiffness afforded by epoxy;

This large emblem, destined to be mounted on a sports stadium, was manufactured using wet lay-up polyester resin and glass fibre

and the carrier fibre can have an even greater effect on thickness. Far less carbon fibre is required to produce the same stiffness as would be provided by the use of glass fibre.

There is a far more important reason for the use of carbon fibres as a carrier material for mould making. Carbon has a very low coefficient of expansion. Therefore, when components of great accuracy are required, a carbon-fibre carrier results in a more thermally-stable mould, that is one that maintains dimensional stability at elevated temperatures, which can be important if elevated-temperature cures or post-cures are to be used. In most cases where the mould is to be used for room-temperature-curing, wet lay-up systems, which are the most widely-used method, then carbon fibre would offer little advantage. The additional cost of using carbon in place of glass fibre would not not be justified.

Up to one third of the total volume of resin could be utilized for the gel coat, unless a manufacturer's gel coat is to be used. Prior to applying the gel coat, the pattern will have to be waxed or treated with some other release agent, as described for solid cast moulds.

The application of the gel coat may be by brush or roller. In some comparatively rare cases, depending on the resin system, the gel coat may be applied in more than one coat, with partial-cure taking place between coats.

When the gel coat has almost cured, at what is known as the 'green' state, the first lamination ply, or layer, can be applied. The carrier for this first ply is usually a tissue, which is a fine, random-fibre material. It can also be used at the time the gel coat is applied, which prevents the gel coat running off the pattern. The tissue also acts as a barrier to prevent loose fibres reaching the mould surface, which can be a problem when chopped-strand mat is being used. This material comprises randomly-placed, short, chopped glass-fibre strands pressed into heavy mat form. It is a very cheap form of carrier which, in the main, is used in low-cost moulds and laminated components. Alternatively, it can be used in conjunction with woven fabric carriers to add thickness.

Chopped-strand mat is not only popular because of its cost, but also for its ease of use; it is very easy to wet out, or saturate, the mat by the resin application, making it quick and easy to work with.

Apart from the type of fibre, that is glass, carbon, etc, there is the style, the thickness of the fibre and the weave to be considered. Plain-weave fabrics are the most common in mould making, but generally weave style is not an over-important consideration. In fact, on lots of moulds, to save cost, only chopped-strand is used, but woven fabric will produce a stiffer and stronger mould for the same weight of glass. This is due to the continuity of fibre.

Subsequent lamination layers are added to the pattern, until the required thickness has been achieved. More than one layer of carrier can be applied with the same mix of resin, as it is not imperative to allow each layer to cure or part-cure before adding the next.

There is, of course, a limit to the amount of resin that can be used in one application, if the exotherm situation is to be avoided. The pot life stated in the manufacturer's instructions will be a good guide. For example, if the pot life is less than an hour, the wet applied thickness should not exceed a thickness of approximately 5 mm; when the pot life is two hours or more, the wet applied thickness is almost unlimited. However, this should only be taken as a guide, as there are almost unlimited permutations of resins and hardeners with differing speeds. Specified information is always available from the manufacturer.

If the selected resin system is an epoxy, the lamination sequence is similar, but more attention will have to be paid to the amount of wet resin applied from the same mix. Although, in many cases, the pot life of epoxy-resin systems is much longer than polyesters, they can be more susceptible to exotherm problems. Therefore, allowing a cure or part-cure between applications of the laminated layers becomes more important. Again, it will depend on the resin and, more importantly, the hardener.

Epoxy resins are very versatile and lend themselves to modification. This results in many base resins, with various compatible hardeners for each resin. Each hardener will have been developed for a specific technical reason. This means that it is possible to select a system that suits the planned application, and can therefore eliminate some of the handling problems.

Epoxy laminations generally take much longer than polyester laminations of similar thicknesses; and epoxy resins are several times the cost of polyesters. Therefore, if epoxy resins are chosen, their technical advantages should justify the additional cost.

Apart from the gel coat, the lamination should not be allowed to become too resin rich or, in fact, too dry. Aim to achieve an approximately 50:50 ratio of resin to fibre by weight. This is not too difficult to achieve. The fibre weight should be known; if not, measure out the amount required and weigh it. Then use approximately the same weight of resin, but remember you will need to mix a little more resin to allow for the residue left in mixing vessels and brushes, etc. If you find yourself running short of resin, you can mix more and finish the lamination without problems, provided this additional resin is utilized before the previous mix has begun to cure.

With the selection of the resin system best suited to the planned application, and a suitable fibre fabric, or fabrics—it may be advantageous to use fine-weave fabric next to the gel coat to give the mould a stiff, crack-resistant quality, with heavier fabrics, or chopped-strand material, as a back-up to add bulk and thickness where necessary—it should be possible to produce excellent laminated moulds using the basic principles laid out in this book.

Having completed the lamination, it is necessary, in most cases, to support the mould in some way. This prevents it becoming distorted, and thus prevents misshapen components. Also, moulds that can flex too much are susceptible to cracking.

In most cases, the mould supports can be made from some form of

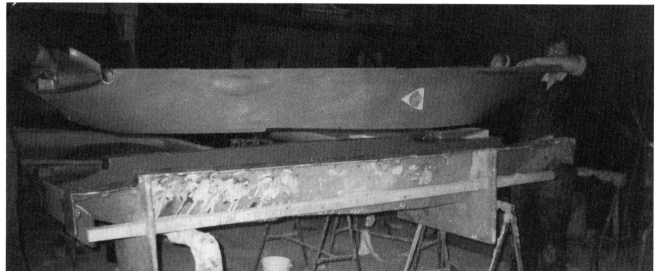

flat, board-like material, the most widely used being plywood, but it can be a composite sandwich board. On moulds where absolute stability is critical, the board from which the mould supports are made can be a thick lamination, at least 15 mm, of the same materials from which the mould is laminated.

The normal method of making mould supports is to cut profiles from the board to fit the shape of the lamination while it is still on the pattern, that is female profiles from rectangular boards. These profiles are placed at intervals along the mould, the spacing depending on the size of the mould. Their ends are then joined by two other boards secured by nails or screws to form a box-like frame. This holds the profiles in place while the final stage takes place.

The final stage is to laminate the profiles to the mould, using the same resin and carrier as for the mould itself. Some mould makers apply one or two layers of fibre fabric along the length of the profile; others add wide bonds at intervals; but the important point is to laminate resin and fibre to the entire length of the profile where it makes contact with the back of the mould. This lamination should take the form of a fillet to fill the angle between the mould surface and the vertical profile.

When cured, the framework laminated to the back of the mould not only serves to stabilize and strengthen the mould, but also acts as a flat base for it.

Profiled boards can also serve another important purpose, and that is to provide the joint faces on a split line where a mould is made in sections.

To produce the mould in sections a dam, or divider, is built up on the pattern in the position of the intended split. Thin plywood or similar material is ideal for this purpose. Part of the mould is then laminated up to this divider, which should be treated with release agent like the rest of the mould. When that part of the mould is cured, the divider is removed, and the exposed edge, or flange, of the freshly-laminated mould section has release agent applied to it. Then the next, or remaining section of the mould is laminated.

The profiled boards can be laminated into the mould-section mating flanges to stiffen them, and in most cases, the split mould sections are bolted back together through the stiffened, laminated flanges.

When the mould is fully cured, its removal from the pattern should be straightforward. If the mould has been made in sections, as is often the case with laminated moulds, removal is much easier. Where the moulds are large in area with limited section, compressed air is sometimes used to assist removal. This can be applied by easing a blunt implement under the edge of the mould, then blowing the air into the gap between the mould and pattern.

If the mould is to be very thick, it is advisable to incorporate some form of air inlet in the mould surface to provide a direct connection for an air line. In very large moulds, several air inlets may be needed. This will not only assist in the removal of the mould from the pattern, but also the subsequent component from the mould.

TOP LEFT Simple laminated polyester components undergoing room-temperature cure

CENTRE LEFT Removing a polyester race-car body from the mould

LEFT Note the use of timber supports, put in as an aid during removal from the mould

Subject to cleaning and polishing, the mould is now ready to produce the first laminated component. Where sectional moulds are used, the sections are usually bolted together.

There is another type of mould used in wet laminating, although whether use of the term 'mould' is correct in this case is debatable, as it could be described as a pattern. It is not made by wet lay-up, but rather from a high-melting-point wax material, developed for use where hollow laminated components are required.

The method by which this type of mould or pattern is utilized consists of producing a shape around which the component can be laminated by wet lay-up. It is necessary to produce a pattern of the required internal shape by the method described for normal mould making. Then a mould is made, covering all sides of the pattern.

When the mould has been removed from the pattern, and the mould sections bolted back together, the mould wax is melted and poured through holes formed at one of the split lines. When the wax has cooled, the mould can be removed, leaving an internal mould in wax.

Wet lay-up components

As with laminated mould making, the basic method for making a component by wet lay-up is similar with most resin types; the main differences occur where cures are more critical, pot life is short, there is a risk of exotherm, the maximum thickness to be applied at one time is limited, or there are other special considerations or instructions from the resin manufacturer. The mould should be fully prepared, including the application of a release agent, preferably one recommended by the manufacturer of the resin system to be used for the laminated component.

The resin system and type will be selected to suit the application, the main considerations being technical performance, cost, or ease of use.

With laminated components, in most cases, the fibre type and weave play a more important part than with mould making. The main consideration is the performance requirement from the finished component. This, of course, can be coupled with cost consideration. For example, if component stiffness is the ultimate aim, then some form of carbon fibre would be the obvious choice; but if cost was a stumbling block, then glass would be selected. To achieve the best possible stiffness from this fibre, the type of fibre and the weave would have to be optimized.

As can be seen from the glass types described earlier in the book, choice of fibre can be a major factor in reaching a performance target, and this can be enhanced by the selection of the most suitable weave style. Weave styles that have the minimum of fibre distortion, such as plain weaves, will be selected if stiffness is the important requirement. However, as previously stated, some of the more intricate weave styles are more drapable and, therefore, more suitable and easier to laminate into components of complex shape. Any stiffness lost through weave distortion is compensated for by the stiffness inherent in the more complex shape of the component.

For high-performance laminated structures, particularly where, in fact, performance is a specific requirement, it is advantageous to make up the fibre weight, or laminate thickness, by using several thin layers of fibre rather than a few thick or heavy fibres.

As with mould making, the component will require a gel coat, particularly if a good surface finish is important. It is very important to ensure that the gel coat remains within the maker's recommended thickness. An over-thick gel coat can lead to surface cracking on the finished component, particularly if it is a thin laminate that will be subject to flexing during use.

Normally, the gel coat is applied by brush or roller, but in some cases, on very large moulds, spraying is possible. However, the relatively high viscosity of gel coats, together with the anti-run fillers added to them, make spraying very difficult.

Another method of preventing the gel coat from running is by the use

Shown here is a ship's deck section being prepared for the addition of stiffening members. The flat area has already been laminated and these two men are shaping foam as a core to form the stiffening section

This photograph shows a panel where the foam cores have been coated with a sealing resin layer

A similar panel where the final lamination has been applied. Note where trimming has been started in the foreground; the finished laminate thickness can be seen. This thickness, as with all other areas, will have been designed to meet the required performance level

A general view of a large deck panel having stiffening sections applied; the flat panel area was made first

The inside of a hull section where stiffening members are being laminated over foam formers. Note the extent of the fume and particle extraction pipes

ABOVE LEFT A hull skin being laminated totally by hand, using the wet lay-up method

ABOVE This view of the traversing gantry shows the men on the far side consolidating the applied resin and glass

LEFT Shown here is a much larger hull, still utilizing wet lay-up; but due to the vast size, a purpose-built gantry, that moves in both horizontal and vertical planes, carries the laminators and the special glass fabric dispenser

This and the following series of photographs show wet lay-up GRP being used in the manufacture of non-metallic ships, and illustrates that this method of manufacture is not limited to small components

of a fibre tissue. The use of a tissue layer is still advisable when a filled gel coat is applied and allowed to cure or part-cure, to serve as the previously-mentioned barrier to prevent the back-up fibres from reaching the component surface. Where a fine woven fabric is used as the carrier, the chances of loose fibres reaching the surface are greatly reduced.

Once the gel coat has reached the stage when it is ready for the next application, the first back-up fibres are laminated on to, or into the mould. If the resin is polyester, and the back-up fibre chopped-strand mat, then several layers, or in some cases all the layers, are put on with the same mix of resin.

One widely-used method of this type of wet laminating is to pre-wet the fibre by putting it into a shallow container of resin and dabbing it with a stiff paint brush, or brushes made for this purpose. This ensures complete saturation of the fibre. The technique may also be carried out on a sheet of polythene instead of in a container. The saturated fibre is then placed in position in, or on, the mould and dabbed firmly all over with the brush or, in many cases, gone over with a ribbed metal roller. In each case, the purpose is to expel the air from the laminate and ensure that it is consolidated. Each layer is processed in this way, regardless of whether they are applied all at once with one mix, or individually and allowed to cure or part-cure before application of the next.

Many laminators, particularly where polyester resin and coarse, open-weave fabrics or chopped-strand mat are being used, wet out the fibres directly on, or in, the mould. It is usual to apply a liberal coat of resin on to the cured gel coat, after which the dry fabric is placed into position. Then more resin is applied and dabbed or rolled in.

With fine- or close-weave fabrics, or where higher-viscosity resins are being used, it is advisable to pre-wet the fibre weave as described.

This basic process will follow similar lines when epoxy or other resins are being used. However, expoxy resins can have very reactive hardeners, which means that there is a danger of exotherm. This will not be a problem

A polyester component being laminated. Note the heavy chopped-strand glass fibre

The lamination awaiting cure at room temperature

The finished component after removal from the mould

if the manufacturer's instructions are followed, too much resin is not applied from the same mix, and each layer is allowed to reach a sufficiently advanced or cured state before the application of the next.

Although epoxy systems can have very reactive hardeners, but this is not always the case, the cure time may still be long. This can make the laminating process a much longer and more complex procedure, but the performance required from the component may make the use of epoxy an automatic choice.

Where phenolic resins are to be used, the basic laminating process will be similar to the use of polyester and epoxy but, in most cases, there will be no suitable gel coat available. Therefore, the required finish will have to be applied as a final stage to the cured component after removal from the mould.

When used as laminating resins, phenolics generally do not have anything like as good a mechanical performance as the other resin systems mentioned. Consequently, they are not used as widely.

However, phenolics can have one outstanding aspect of performance, and this is their fire-retardant properties. Phenolics have a natural resistance to burning, and by added modification this property can be enhanced.

Another very desirable feature of phenolics is that, if they are subjected to temperatures high enough to degrade or char them (this means temperatures of 500–600°C, or even higher), the fumes given off are lower in volume and of much lower toxic level than any other laminating resins in general use.

These very special properties render this family of resins suitable for laminating a particular range of components. One prime example, where they are utilized to the full, is aircraft interiors, that is panel surfaces, galley structures etc. They also have uses in non-aerospace passenger-carrying vehicles; for ducting or components used in high-temperature environments; and as a safety aspect in competition vehicles.

As explained previously, phenolics have much lower inherent strength as laminating resins compared with the other resin systems described. Consequently, this point must be considered when phenolics are being utilized.

If the component is to be a non-structural panel, that is a self-supporting, fire-retardant surface, or some form of ducting or similar moulding, then phenolics can be used as a straight laminate. However, if the fire-retardant qualities of a phenolic are required in a load-bearing structure, or the phenolic is to be used as a facing skin or on a sandwich panel, then other steps must be taken to ensure sufficient strength in the finished component.

If the component is a load-bearing, normal laminate, that is there is no sandwich core material, then the laminate will have to be designed with sufficient bulk, or thickness, to compensate for the lower structural performance. Where a sandwich core material, such as honeycomb, is used, the lower stiffness of the phenolic has to be overcome, if extremely thick facing skins are to be avoided. In addition, phenolic does not bond or adhere to core materials as well as epoxy resin systems.

Epoxy resins are ideal for use in conjunction with phenolic resins to overcome the shortcomings of the latter when used on their own. The former are laminated in sufficient layers to achieve the required mechanical performance. Then the outer layers are applied using phenolic, which gives the finished laminate its flame-retardant properties.

The flame-retardant properties of this type of multi-resin laminate are restricted to surface-spread-of-flame and short-time flame exposure. However, where the laminate is subjected to temperatures high enough to char or burn it, the epoxy resin will give off both smoke and toxic gases.

In many cases, surface-spread-of-flame is the specified requirement, as this type of resistance is considered to give sufficient time in a fire for evacuation; but the lack, or limited amount, of smoke and very low toxic yield resulting from a totally-phenolic laminate must eventually lead to the material's more widespread use as regulations demand.

Where epoxy and phenolic resins are to be cured together, the process must be given close attention. The actual method by which this type of hybrid laminate is manufactured will depend, to a great degree, on the systems being used. It is not possible to give specific details on all the possible resins and their handling details.

The differing methods of curing phenolics must be considered when they are being used in conjunction with resins of an entirely different chemical nature.

The main method of curing phenolics is by thermosetting, that is a simple elevated-temperature cure. However, this type of cure does not lend itself to general use within a wet lay-up resin system. This is because a phenolic cured in this manner produces a small percentage of water vapour during the elevated-temperature cure. This, in turn, generates internal pressure in the resin. To utilize this form of phenolic, pressure is applied during the cure; to produce sufficient pressure, and this can mean up to 50 psi or more, matched tooling may be required. In many cases, this can mean very expensive metal tools, but for some special components requiring the performance this method can produce, the expense is justified.

When the elevated-temperature cure is used in conjunction with wet lay-up, the actual laminating process is a simple matter of wetting out the selected fibre and building up the layers to produce the required thickness. With matched tools, it must be remembered that the mould must be slightly over-filled so that the laminate is compressed when the two halves of the mould are closed together.

With this type of phenolic, it is important to follow the manufacturer's curing instructions so that an exotherm situation does not occur.

The most widely-used method of curing wet lay-up, phenolic laminating resin systems is by the use of acid activating catalysts, or hardeners. These types of catalyst, or hardener, are usually of a slow and low-reactive nature. This allows sufficient laminating time.

Although complete cures are possible using acid-type catalysts, or hardeners, it is far more common for the catalyst to produce an advanced stage of cure. Full performance of the system is achieved by the use of an elevated-temperature post-cure, and in most cases this can be carried out with the component removed from the mould. This is a very important point, as it means that the maximum performance can be obtained from the phenolic without the need for expensive, high-temperature-resistant tooling or moulds.

The laminating process for this type of curing system is straightforward, being the same as for the previously-described wet laminating.

Phenolics cured by the reactive-hardener method tend to have long pot lives, which can make laminating with these materials a long process. This is not an absolute rule, however, and pot life and cure times will vary with different manufacturers, who will modify and vary both resin and catalyst.

Another method of curing resin from the same chemical family is by exposure to ultra-violet light. Because of the nature of the cure, this form is best suited to thin applications, such as gel coats. These are usually very thin layers applied to prevent surface porosity.

The main advantage of this method is speed. When these very thin applications are exposed to strong ultra-violet light, in some cases, the cure time can be seconds.

This type of gel coat is not widely used, partly due to the need for very thin applications and partly the fact that special ultra-violet equipment is required to effect the cure. Furthermore, it has limited advantages to offer the wet laminating technique.

Gel coats are not generally used as often with phenolics as with other laminating-resin systems. Surface finishes are often applied to the finished component as a final operation; to maintain the fire-retardant properties, in many cases, the final finish will be one of the paints specially developed for this type of application.

Wet laminating is a very practical, and comparatively simple, method of producing a very wide range of composite components. Some components, however, can be of very complex nature and will require the skill of an experienced laminator, but these skills can be gained by working on simple parts to begin with.

In many cases, the materials utilized in wet laminating are comparatively simple to use, but some may require very close attention to the manufacturer's instructions or handling by experienced personnel. This may be because a high level of skill is required or because special precautions are needed from a health and safety point of view. For example, some resins can be prone to exotherm reaction, as previously described, or can cause skin irritations, in some cases dermatitis, so care should always be taken. Relevant warnings will always be part of the manufacturer's literature. Provided these instructions are adhered to, all the products can be utilized without undue danger.

3 Dry laminating

This now widely used and still fast growing method of producing resin-and-fibre laminated components is carried out using pre-pregs. The term 'pre-preg' applies to fibre, in many cases woven into fabrics, pre-impregnated with the matrix-resin system which, in almost all cases, is of the elevated-temperature-curing type.

The fibres for this type of material can be of almost any type, that is carbon, Kevlar, glass, boron etc. Also, any selected weave style can be used for most of these fibres, with the exception of boron, the exceptional fibre stiffness of which limits the possible fibre distortion and, therefore, its suitability for weaving. Due to this, and other technical reasons, boron has limited, but specialized, applications and is not as readily available as the more widely used fibre types.

Boron fibres are also quite hazardous to work with. Being extremely stiff, the fibres will penetrate the skin to great depth. In addition, they are very toxic. Therefore, if the application is specialized enough to demand boron fibres, it is advisable that the component be manufactured by an experienced pre-preg laminator.

There are many advantages to dry pre-preg laminating. The term 'dry pre-preg' is used, despite the fact that some pre-pregs are tacky. In most cases, when the material has a tacky surface, it is intentional and is to assist in the lay-up stage, so that the pre-preg will hold itself in place in a deep-sided or complicated mould. To achieve this, the amount of tack is not very pronounced.

Other more tacky pre-pregs are those using resin systems that have a low-temperature curing capability. These are usually epoxy resins derived from modified room-temperature-curing systems, or similar chemical types, and have to remain very tacky to be usable and have as much usable life as possible. Even then, the shelf life, that is the time the material remains usable after manufacture, is very short, and may be a matter of weeks or even less. The proper elevated-temperature-curing systems generally have a much longer life, from several months upwards, when stored at sub-zero temperatures. A household chest freezer is ideal.

The question of storage life and shelf or bench life will vary considerably with different chemical systems, and may also be affected by the many modifications that the manufacturers carry out to enhance some specific aspect or to produce a material to meet most technical requirements, or a cost requirement or processing capability. On occasion, some form of compromise must be made, but with pre-preg materials the choice is much wider than with those for wet laminating.

Dry laminating using pre-pregs enables the designer and laminator to achieve the optimum performance from the selected materials, which becomes a more important advantage when the planned component is a load-bearing structure. This latter point is confirmed by the fact that aircraft and race-car constructors, among many others, have utilized pre-preg materials for the manufacture of structural composite components.

Consistency is the key word when using pre-preg materials, and is very important if design requirements are to be maintained.

Included under the consistency heading is a constant weight. Pre-pregs usually maintain a specific weight, due to a known weight of woven fabric being impregnated with a controlled amount of matrix resin for a given area. This enables the pre-preg manufacturer to control the resin-to-fibre ratio, which can be very important if the potential performance of any pre-preg is to be utilized. For example, technical performance may have an effect on the storage and bench life. Therefore, all these points should be considered when selecting materials; in most cases, however, it is the performance requirement, or cost, that is the major contributing factor in the selection of laminating materials.

Another important point when selecting pre-preg materials is the cure capabilities of the available processing equipment. Is the oven or autoclave capable of reaching a high enough temperature, especially if a pre-preg from the higher-temperature range is required? These are in the 175–200°C band, and it is important to remember that the mould can be of considerable bulk that must also be elevated to the cure temperature.

Also very important when using elevated-temperature-curing pre-pregs are the tooling, or mould-making materials. These will have to withstand a temperature of at least the same as, or ideally higher than the cure temperature of the pre-preg that will be processed in the tool or mould.

The range of possible pre-pregs from both the chemical aspect and the almost endless selection of variants of each system, result in an available pre-preg range that will achieve the maximum stiffness from a certain fibre, the laminate must not be over-rich in resin. Therefore, if the project in hand is a multi-layer laminate, the resin content of the pre-preg needs to be lower to prevent the build-up of excess resin, although this can be overcome; more on that point later. If, on the other hand, the laminated pre-preg is to form the skin of a sandwich panel, additional resin will be needed to form the adhesive bond between skin and core material.

As a guide, pre-pregs to be used for multi-layer laminates will, in many cases, have a resin content of a little over 30 per cent; for sandwich panels, however, the resin content is usually 40 per cent or more. These are not golden rules, and each design will utilize the most suitable pre-preg coupled with technique to achieve the desired performance or appearance.

The last point is one example where high-resin-content pre-preg is sometimes used in a multi-layer laminate, and that is to produce a resin-rich surface, which results in a dense, non-porous skin of excellent appearance. To achieve this it may only be necessary to use the material for the first one or two layers, that is those that are the first layers into, or on to, the mould. Using this technique not only produces an excellent surface, but does so without the need for a gel coat.

Some types of weave and some types of pre-preg, usually due to the resin, give an excellent mechanical performance, but do not produce an ultra-smooth finish. There is a method to overcome the problem, which will be described later.

Pre-pregs, in the main being elevated-temperature curing, will require tooling or moulds that are capable of withstanding the temperatures involved. This means that the temperature resistance of the mould should be higher than the actual cure temperature of the selected pre-preg, especially if the tool or mould is to be used repeatedly.

Where the tool, or mould, is to be used once only, as in the case of a prototype component, cheaper resin systems can be considered. The main point to watch is that if some cold-curing resin systems used for tooling or mould making are subjected to elevated temperatures, the mould can soften. This can lead to distortion and deterioration of the mould surface, causing the moulded component to stick and be difficult to remove. This also can result in a component with a poor surface finish.

In most cases where elevated-temperature-curing pre-pregs are to be used for the laminated component, the chosen tooling resin will be epoxy, because of its stability and its ability to withstand the higher-temperature cures. However, polyester should not be ruled out, as now there are more grades available that are quite good at elevated temperature, and with polyesters the cost is usually lower.

Dry, or pre-preg, laminating is not confined to the actual laminated component. Pre-pregs are also supplied in forms suitable for tool, or mould, making, the advantages being material control, that is the ratio of resin to fibre is controlled at levels to give the optimum performance. This can be a great advantage to the less-experienced operator, who would have difficulty in achieving similar control using wet laminating techniques. Furthermore, the use of pre-pregs is much cleaner from the handling aspect which, in some cases, can also mean less risk from dermatitis and other skin irritations. This does not mean, of course, that wet laminating cannot be carried out safely.

For technical reasons, some resin systems are known to be very dermatitic, but when handled correctly, following the manufacturer's instructions and warnings, they produce excellent products safely.

When manufacturing a tool, or mould, using pre-preg materials, the pattern on which the mould is based will be made in the same manner, basically, as for a wet-laminated tool or mould.

The prepared pattern will require treating with a release agent, but it must be remembered that the mould will be cured at elevated temperature and, therefore, the release agent must be suitable for the planned temperature range. Most of the available standard release agents are designed for this purpose. However, the standard mould waxes, as used for room-temperature-curing wet laminating, should not be employed.

After the pattern has been prepared for a mould using pre-preg materials, the final decision prior to commencing the laminating is whether or not to apply a gel coat. Until recent years the use of gel coats with elevated-temperature cures of 120°C and above was rare; many laminated components, and some moulds, are still produced without the use of gel coats.

If a gel coat is to be used, it must be designed for, or be capable of being cured at, the temperature of the back-up laminating pre-preg.

There are two main types of gel coat for use in conjunction with pre-pregs. One is an epoxy resin which is applied in a similar manner to wet lay-up gel coats, i.e. by brush in most cases. Then it is allowed to part-cure at room temperature, after which the pre-preg is laminated on to the gel coat. Finally, the cure for both pre-preg and gel coat takes place at elevated temperature.

The other common gel coat used with pre-pregs consists of phenolic resin modified to be compatible with epoxy pre-pregs. Another clever modification produces two curing systems in the one resin. The gel coat is applied in the same way as any other, and one curing system causes it to part-cure after exposure to strong ultra-violet light. Lamination of the pre-preg follows and the gel coat achieves its full cure at elevated temperature with the pre-preg. This type of gel coat is usually applied as a very thin coat and is intended mainly to overcome the surface porosity that is persistent with the use of some types of pre-preg. In most cases, it is not suitable as a thick, dense surface to mould a component like a normal gel coat.

As with wet laminating, it is possible to use colour pigments in the gel coat to produce a ready-coloured component. This does not work very well in the case of phenolics, due to the colour changing at elevated temperatures, but excellent results can be obtained with epoxy resins and pre-pregs. Resin manufacturers will recommend pigment types and mixing ratios.

Another method of obtaining a self-coloured finish is to use standard two-part epoxy paint as a gel coat. Trials on coating thickness should be carried out to achieve even colour distribution without having to apply too thick a coat. These trials will also establish whether the selected paint and resin are compatible under the conditions in which the project is to be processed.

With the pattern prepared and the gel coat applied, lamination can begin. In most cases, this is carried out before the gel coat has cured completely. The material data sheet will give precise details.

For mould making, the pre-preg will be a woven version of the selected fibre type. It may be a finer, light weave style for the first few layers, if the pattern is of very complex shape, followed by heavier material to add the bulk. If the shape does not have tight curves or corners, the heavier material can be used throughout.

It will be unlikely that each layer of pre-preg can be applied as one piece of material matching the area of the pattern. This, of course, depends on the shape. It is more common, therefore, to tailor several pieces to make up the area.

Before beginning, it is advisable to cut the laminating pre-preg into pieces of a convenient and manageable size or shape. When cutting the material to a specific shape to fit the pattern—and this will be an important point when laying up the component itself, as you will need to keep the pre-preg overlaps even—it is worth making cutting templates. These are made from thin paper or some form of cloth, which is held over the pattern and marked for shape, then cut and trimmed until it fits part of the pattern. When the required number of templates have been cut, they can be used to mark out the pre-preg. Alternatively, the shapes can be transferred to a stiffer material, such as card or thin aluminium. This not only makes them suitable for repeated use, but also has the added advantage that they can be used for the direct cutting out of the pre-preg shapes.

As previously stated for mould making, fibre direction is not usually a major concern. It is important, however, to consider the balance of the fibre direction, and you should aim to have equal amounts of fibre running in all directions. This will give increased stability to the mould if it is to be used at elevated temperatures.

The mould shape will determine, to some extent, where the lay-up begins. There are no golden rules on this point, but it is important to make a note of the number of layers as they are applied. It is very easy to lose count when a large number of layers, such as used in mould making, are to be applied. It also helps to ensure that the pieces that make up a complete layer are all placed correctly, which is important to ensure that the mould thickness is constant. This ensures greater stability when the mould is subjected to elevated temperature.

If the pre-preg is of a tacky type, application of the first layer on to the pattern will be straightforward, as the tackiness will hold the pre-preg in place.

Most woven pre-pregs will have some drapability, that is they can be stretched or compressed to fit the shape of the male or female pattern. The basic method is to stretch the pre-preg taut over, or into the pattern, using the pre-cut pieces; to ensure the pre-preg is in close contact with the pattern, local pressure must be exerted. This can be done with spatula-type tools that are usually home-made and have shapes to suit the person doing the laminating. These spatulas are used to press the pre-preg into close contact with the open areas of the pattern, but in particular into the tight corners and areas of complex shape.

Another very useful method of consolidating pre-preg is by the use of a small ridged roller. These can be purchased ready-made, but many laminators make their own by assembling metal washers of two different sizes (approximately 15 mm diameter and some smaller) on to a metal rod, which is bent at right angles. The smaller washers serve as spacers between the larger ones. With a handle fixed to the free end of the rod, an excellent consolidating roller is produced. This is used to force the pre-preg into close contact with all areas of the pattern's surface, especially the tight corners.

The choice of spatula or roller is dependent on the laminator's preference and the job in hand, but there may be certain circumstances where either method is equally suitable for the shape.

If the pre-preg being used is not tacky, the universal method of making it stick to the pattern is by the use of a warm-air blower, which is rather like an industrial version of a hair drier. This is simply used to warm the pre-preg locally, producing a temporary tack to hold the pre-preg in place; in the case of the first layer, you can warm the surface of the pattern locally as you apply the pre-preg.

The use of localized heat will assist throughout the lamination. However, one very important point is that the pre-preg temperature must not be allowed to rise too high, otherwise the resin will begin to gel, which would seriously affect its performance. If the pre-preg is a 120°C curing system, the warm-up temperature should not exceed 70°C. As a guide, this is about the limit a person can hold.

With low-temperature curing systems, that is usually below 90°C, these resins normally cure by a different chemical method and are, in most cases, very tacky by nature, so no additional heat is required. Sometimes this extra tackiness can be a problem, making it difficult to lift one piece of pre-preg from another to move or reposition it. Therefore, care must be taken to place each piece of pre-preg in the correct position before carrying out a roller or spatula consolidation.

Each layer, or ply, is applied, then consolidated on to the previous layer, or ply. This consolidation is a very important part of mould making, preventing the formation of voids, which becomes more difficult as the number of layers increases.

There is a technique used when laminating by this method known as debulking. This consists of applying pressure to the lay-up by the use of vacuum. It is carried out by putting the whole pattern and part-laminated mould into a plastic bag, which is sealed with some form of vacuum take-off attached to a vacuum pump. While the vacuum is being pulled, the plastic vacuum bag is tucked into all the corners and detail of the pattern. This results in an all-over pressure of one atmosphere.

The debulking process consolidates the pre-preg layers, helps to eliminate voids and ensures that the full detail of the pattern is reproduced.

The vacuum-bag material is a temperature-resistant plastic sheet, or diaphragm, produced by many suppliers, some offering differing thicknesses. The thinner the material, the easier it will be to handle, but with very large components, needing a large vacuum bag, it may be advisable to use a thicker material. However, it must be remembered that whatever vacuum-bag material is used, it must follow very closely the contours and tight corners of the lamination.

The point at which debulking takes place will depend to some extent, on the type of pre-preg being used, that is its thickness. As a guide, where the overall mould wall thickness is to be in the region of 6 mm, debulking would take place four times.

When sufficient layers have been laminated for the first debulk, the lamination is covered with a release film. This is a very thin plastic that prevents the resin from sticking to the next layer of material, which is the air-bleed layer. This is a thick, low-density material designed to prevent the vacuum bag from sealing off and preventing all the air being evacuated. It also protects the vacuum bag from damage against any sharp edges or corners.

Once under vacuum, the lamination is maintained in this condition for up to one hour, which allows the pre-preg to settle into all the pattern details and become fully consolidated.

With some pre-preg types, the lamination is warmed while still under vacuum. This aids consolidation by making the resin more mobile. Care must be taken, however, not to let the temperature reach the gel temperature of the resin. With 120°C curing systems, or above, the warm-up temperature should not exceed 70°C. With very-low-temperature curing systems, the resins are usually very tacky and, therefore, very mobile, so a warm-up period is not necessary.

Once the mould wall has been built up to the required thickness, the lamination is placed under vacuum once again for the final cure of the pre-preg.

The optimum cure temperature and time will be stated on the resin's technical data sheet. To assist in the accurate control of this vital temperature, it is advisable, and normal practice, to record the cure temperature direct from a point in, or close to, the resin itself. This can be achieved by the use of an electronic thermometer.

The procedure is to use a thermocouple, which is simply a thin, twin-core wire, the ends of which are twisted or soldered together. This joined end is put into, or on, the resin laminate itself, while the other end is attached to the terminals of the thermometer. By this method, it is possible to monitor the rate of temperature rise, which can be important, as some resin systems have a specified rate of temperature increase.

Electronic thermometers can vary from simple hand-held instruments to very complex and comprehensive, programmable types with autographic temperature record. The latter may be necessary with some types of contract, such as in the aerospace industry. It is inadvisable to rely on a standard oven thermometer, which records the air temperature, not that of the resin, as it will not indicate when the resin is at cure temperature. This makes it difficult to time the cure accurately.

With the thermocouple in place, the pre-preg lamination is covered with release film, cut and tailored to fit as neatly as possible, as this will be the finished outer surface of the mould. This does not affect the perform-

An accurate check of temperature can be made using a hand-held instrument, as shown here, but some can give an autographic record or be linked directly into the temperature control system

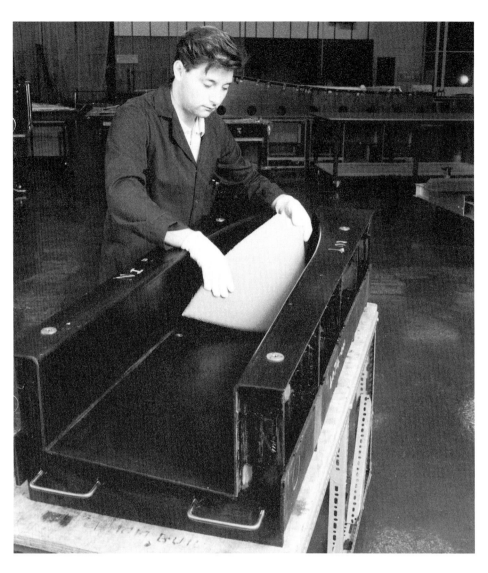

A typical mould. Note the flange width

ance of the mould, but it does help general appearance. After the release film, a layer of air-bleed mat is added to assist the extraction of the air. This is followed by the vacuum bag itself.

The vacuum bag can be utilized in a choice of two ways. One is to totally enclose the pattern and lamination, although some moulds may be too large, or too heavy, to manoeuvre into a total-envelope-type vacuum bag. The other method is to provide the mould with a flange on to which the vacuum bag can be sealed. This flange can be formed by placing the pattern on a base and extending the lamination from the pattern on to the base. Alternatively, in the case of a split mould, the same type of flange can be formed by using wider fences, or dividers, than normal, so that there is space outside the laminated mould joining flange to place a strip of vacuum-bag sealing strip.

On this point of flanges, it is important to consider the finished mould and the way in which it is to be used. If it is to be for very simple, wet lay-up components, then flanges on the mould are not necessary. On the other hand if the component is to be made by an expensive, or complex, wet lay-up process, then debulking, or consolidation by vacuum, may form part of the process and, therefore, extra-wide mould flanges are an important consideration.

Flange width to take a vacuum seal should be at least 25 mm, but 50 mm is more practical. The flange must run around the entire perimeter of the mould. Any corners or acute changes of flange direction should not cause a problem, as the vacuum seal is a very flexible, putty-like material, which can follow almost any route.

When making the vacuum bag, a strip of sealing material should be placed around the mould flange. The bag itself should be made from a sheet of material much larger than the mould. Quite how much larger is dependent on the depth or complexity of the mould, but it is important that the vacuum bag has plenty of spare material.

The purpose of having excess vacuum-bag material is to prevent the bag from bridging corners or angles. If the bag bridges any point so that it does not make contact with the lamination at that point, no pressure will be applied during the cure cycle. This will result in an unconsolidated area which, in turn, could cause a breakout.

A breakout is a void just under the gel coat, which may not be visible when the mould is removed from the pattern, but could collapse during the laminating of a component. This may only produce a surface blemish on the component, but could be serious enough to cause it to become locked in the mould.

In many cases, these breakouts show themselves when the new mould is passed through another cure cycle. If time allows, a second post-cure will show up any surface breakouts or blisters, and will also help to age the mould, which can assist dimensional stability. This later stage of second curing is not essential in all cases; time and job quality are the deciding factors.

If the laminated pre-preg mould is a sectional one, the flanges at the joins between the sections will have to be drilled for the clamp bolts before the mould is removed from the pattern, otherwise accurate alignment of the sections will be difficult.

One useful aid to alignment of the sections, whether pre-drilled or not, is to drill countersinks into the flange faces of each section when a fence, or separator, is removed prior to laminating the next section. The latter will then have corresponding raised bosses on its mating flange. This method can also be used on wet lay-up moulds.

On large moulds, metal pegs with receivers are moulded into the mould joining flanges to serve as the same form of positive location aid.

With the mould released from the pattern and the sections bolted back together, all that remains is to check for any small undercuts or rough areas, which must be removed and polished. Cutting compound used to polish paint on car bodywork is an ideal material for this purpose. Next, a suitable release agent is applied and the mould is ready for lamination of the first component.

4 Component manufacture by pre-preg lamination

FABRIC TAILORING METHODS

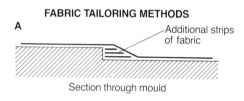

Section through mould

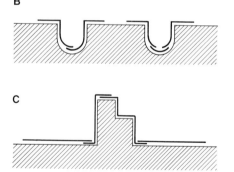

A The use of additional fabric helps to provide full and sharp corners on the finished component
B This method of cutting the fabric allows for slippage and ensures that the fabric follows all the mould detail
C This also allows for slippage and assists tailoring the fabric over complex mould protrusions

Components manufactured using pre-preg materials can be as simple to make, and very similar in method, as laminated moulds. However, they can also be very complex, either because the mould shape is complicated, or the pre-pregs chosen are more difficult to manipulate.

In some cases, where ultimate performance is not essential, the pre-pregs chosen can be the simplest to use for the shape. Where the fibre direction is not important, the lamination is comparatively straightforward and simple, and very much like the procedure for laminated mould making.

The choice of pre-preg for the component is usually far more comprehensive than that for mould making. There are many more weave types and weights, different fibre types, and a much wider choice of resins; all these, plus the combinations offered by the many suppliers, add up to a very wide potential choice indeed.

There are, of course, unidirectional pre-pregs that add yet another potential material choice. The fibres of these particular pre-pregs are not woven, but impregnated with resin as straight fibres. Various fibre types are impregnated in this way. The reasons for this range of pre-pregs and their uses are described later.

There is no golden rule as to where laminating should begin on, or in, the mould. The mould shape will have some bearing on this point, as will the preference of the individual laminator. Even experienced laminators may choose different points at which to begin.

There are some aspects of the work that all laminators will carry out in a similar fashion. For example, at return flanges or edge reinforcements, strips of pre-preg will be cut to flange width and used to build up the required additional thickness. Narrow strips of pre-preg, or pieces rolled into thin rods, will be tucked into very tight corners or crevices where it is difficult to ensure adequate pressure from the vacuum bag, or to retain the main lamination. This also prevents ugly blowouts or resin-starved areas in these tight spots. This method helps to prevent damage to the pre-preg fibres that can occur when trying to force the material into these

Shown here are the materials used for component manufacture in pre-preg. Note the absence of any liquid resin system. The heater gun is to assist in the lay-up

areas using thin, or sharp, laminating instruments.

Pre-filling tight corners, etc is particularly useful when the component is to be used in the unpainted condition, which is often the case with carbon and Kevlar. When the finished item is to be painted, any small breakouts or surface voids can be filled beforehand.

Where the component has return flanges, to which extra strips of pre-preg are to be added, one useful method is to put a layer of the lamination in the mould. If necessary, this can be assisted by the use of a hot-air blower. The first layer will serve to hold the strips in place, as they will all stick together.

As with making the mould, in some cases, the layers of pre-preg may be put into the mould in one piece or, more often, in sections. Where sections are used, it is always a good idea to keep the necessary overlaps at as constant a width as possible; where the lamination has many layers, the overlaps should not all fall in the same place. There is no golden rule about overlap width, but with most woven pre-pregs, somewhere in the region of 15 mm is ideal.

With both male and female moulds, it is quite common for the laminating process to begin in the middle and work out towards the edges. This can be straightforward when all the pre-preg being used is woven, because the fabric weave allows the pre-preg to drape. This means it can be stretched and distorted to follow the mould contours.

Some weave types are more drapable than others, so the ease with which the pre-preg layers can be applied will depend on the complexity of the mould, or component, shape and the drapability of the pre-preg.

A situation that requires close attention is where unidirectional pre-pregs are being used in a shaped component, adding stiffness to woven material in strategic areas. The additional stiffness offered by unidirectional fibres makes them much more difficult to tailor around compound curves, added to which, as there is no supporting cross-weave, the fibres have a tendency to separate if the pre-preg is not handled carefully. This is the reason why complex shapes are designed for woven materials and,

PRE-PREG LAMINATING TECHNIQUES

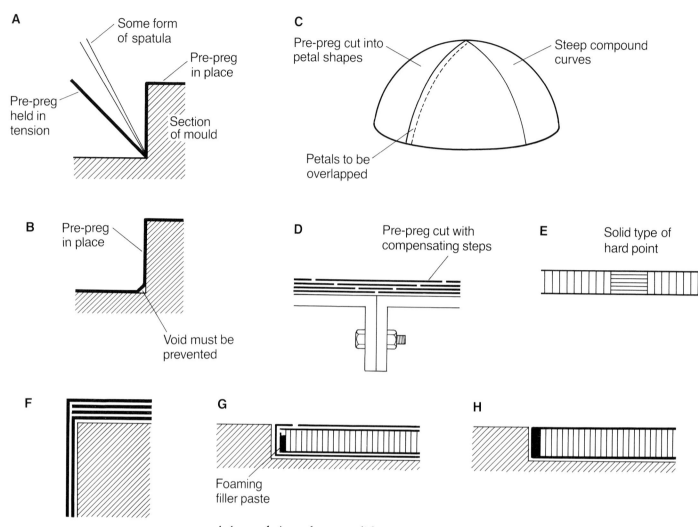

A A spatula is used to consolidate pre-preg into corners
B This method of tailoring pre-preg can be used for female or male mould shapes
C This type of hard point, or insert, is built into sandwich panels at the time of manufacture. It can be layers of pre-preg cured at the same time as the panel, or pre-made into a block prior to the panel lay-up. Other solid metallic or non-metallic materials can be used for this purpose. Inserts of the types fitted after the panel has been completed are shown elsewhere in the book
D Voids at internal corners must be avoided
E The method for joining pre-preg with split moulds
F The use of extra pre-preg for thickening flange areas
G Using pre-preg to form sealed sandwich-panel edges
H Solid pre-made edge members can be moulded in

THE USE OF UNBALANCED WEAVES

A

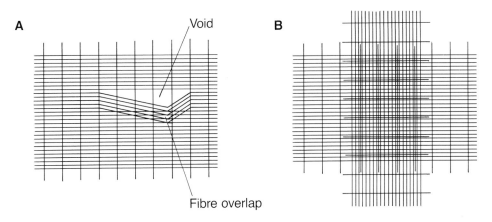

Void

Fibre overlap

B

C

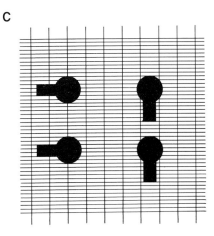

A When the fabric has a much higher percentage of fibre in one direction than the other, care must be taken to prevent the almost free fibre from becoming distorted to prevent voids and added thickness where fibres cross over each other
B With multi-layer laminates from these types of fabric, the layer must be placed at 90 degrees to the previous layer to complete the laminate to the selected thickness. This ensures that the laminate will have the same mechanical performance in both directions
C When cutting shaped layers to produce a multi-layer laminate, rotate the cutting pattern through 90 degrees for each layer to ensure that the laminate has the same mechanical performance in both directions
The above notes do not apply if this type of fabric is being used to achieve a specific mechanical performance in one direction. Bias for weaves with diagonal fibres must be considered using the above notes but with special attention to specific weave styles.

if necessary, unidirectional fibres are added strategically.

Where a component is designed mainly, or totally, for unidirectional pre-preg, the required shape will take the handling qualities of the pre-preg into account.

Apart from the limitations caused by the lack of drapability, unidirec-

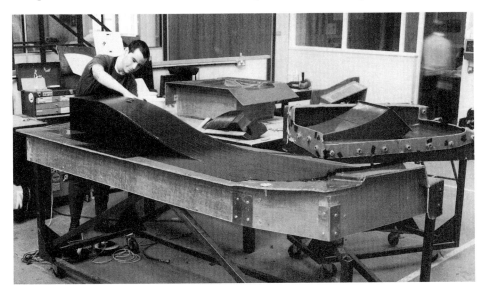

This photograph shows a highly-stressed race-car underside being laid up. To achieve maximum stiffness over its length, unidirectional carbon fibre pre-preg is being used

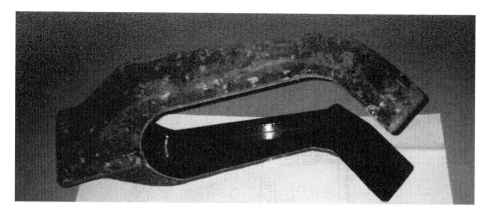

Shown here is a carbon fibre mould made in two parts and bolted together. The component is to be a sandwich structure, and the outer carbon fibre skin lay-up is carried out with the mould unbolted

One half of the mould laid-up and under vacuum. This is to debulk, or consolidate, the pre-preg layers. The process is carried out every few layers and at low temperature, but warm enough to soften the resin without any effect on the ultimate cure

The two separate halves have the outer skin lay-up in place and are then bolted together. A pre-preg splice is carried out at the joint line, and the necessary peel ply, release film and air-bleed layers are put in place. Shown here is the complete mould under vacuum, awaiting transfer to the oven for the cure of the first and outer skin

The resultant sandwich structure in its completed form. The shaped honeycomb was bonded to the cured outer skin, using epoxy film adhesive, at the same time as the cure for the laminated pre-preg inner skin. The various inserts shown in this photograph were bonded in using two-part epoxy adhesive to complete the racing motorcycle chassis

tional pre-pregs are handled in the same basic manner as woven pre-pregs, that is with a hot-air blower and rollers or spatulas.

One of the important points to remember with these types of pre-preg is that because there is no cross-weave to hold the fibres together, it is very easy to force them apart during the laminating process. This must be avoided, if possible, as it can have an adverse effect on the laminate's mechanical performance.

Another major consideration is that there is no stretch in the fibre direction. Therefore, extreme care must be taken to ensure that the pre-preg laying in the fibre direction is carefully compounded into any tight corners as each layer is applied. This is essential, for the debulking process will only consolidate the laminate in the open areas and will not be able to force the unstretchable fibres into corners or tight areas if they have been left bridging any point during the lamination.

On complex shapes, unidirectional pre-pregs do require much more

The finished mould is seen here with part of the pre-preg lay-up in place

The completed component

RIGHT In the foreground a race-car engine cover is being laid up, using pre-preg. The required number of layers are in place and bands of film adhesive have been applied. Note the completed engine cover being removed from the mould in the background. The light area is a heat-reflective layer

BELOW RIGHT The bands of film adhesive serve to hold the non-metallic honeycomb core in place while the second pre-preg skin is applied, resulting in a sandwich structure. The hot-air gun softens the adhesive film and renders it tacky

BOTTOM RIGHT Here is another component having the honeycomb put in place on the first pre-preg skin. Note the contoured shape to which the core is being held

BELOW The finished engine cover is seen here from the outside

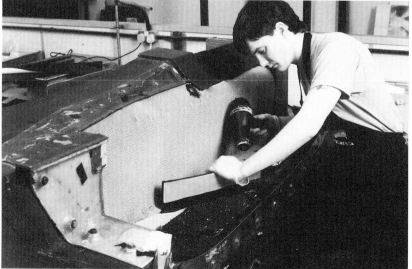

skill and care, but they can be used to great effect if handled correctly.

With the pre-preg, whatever the type or combination of types, laminated to the required thickness, the laminator can move on to the next stage. If the component is a straightforward, simple laminate, the cure would be next, but if the first lamination is to make the outer skin of a sandwich structure, then one of two possible steps is taken.

In some cases, the first laminated skin is placed under vacuum and cured. This method ensures that the lamination is fully consolidated and, therefore, that the full design performance is achieved from the lamination, together with the best possible surface finish.

The alternative step, used in many cases, is to place the honeycomb core directly on to the uncured first skin lamination; the second, or outer, skin is then laminated directly on to the honeycomb.

If the first option is to be the method used and the outer skin lamination is complete, the next and important part of the process is to cover the lamination with a release film. This should be laid on to the pre-preg with as few wrinkles as possible, as they will affect the finished surface to which the honeycomb must be bonded.

In many cases, to assist the production of a flatter surface finish and to produce a slightly roughened finish ideal for the next layer, a peel ply is used. This is a fine woven fabric which can be a nylon-type material or a surface-treated glass. The peel ply is laid on to the lamination. If warmed, the pre-preg will become tacky, which will assist in getting the peel ply to stay in position.

With or without peel ply, the release film is essential. It is followed by the air-bleed layer, which covers the entire area of the component. The complete lay-up is then covered by the vacuum bag.

As previously mentioned, when elevated-temperature cures are to be used, the mould will, in most cases, have built-in flanges on to which the vacuum bag can be sealed. This is achieved with the use of purpose-made, temperature-resistant sealant strip. With this strip placed around the flange, the vacuum bag is simply pressed on to it.

As it is impossible to contour the flat vacuum-bag material to complex shapes, this must be overcome by having the bag much larger than would appear to be required. This means that if you are sealing the bag to a mould flange, the distance around the edge of the bag material is much longer than around the mould. To overcome this you use enforced tucks.

The tucks are made by pressing the bag flat on to the sealer for a short distance, then a short length of sealing tape is placed vertically, or at right angles to the run of the flange. The bag material runs up one side of the tag of sealer and down the other. In effect, in the thickness of the sealer (6 or 8 mm), you have lost as much bag material as the length of the vertical sealer tag.

Sealer tags can be as long as you wish, or you can use as many tags and tucks as you need.

Tucks are also used where the bag has to follow a dramatic change of mould flange shape, that is acute angles or curves. The same sealing

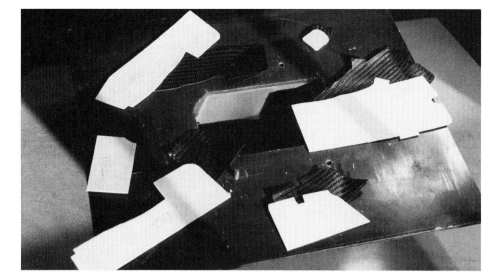

The stages of a typical pre-preg lay-up are shown in this and subsequent photographs. Shown here is a set of pre-preg cutting templates, together with the cut pre-preg, laid out on the mould to be used.

The lay-up being carried out

After application of the mould release, the carbon fibre pre-preg is laid up, using the required number of layers or plies

A peel ply layer in place on the laid up pre-preg. This is peeled from the completed component, together with any excess resin that has bled through. The resultant surface has a smooth, matt finish that is free from resin runs and is ideal for painting or secondary bonding

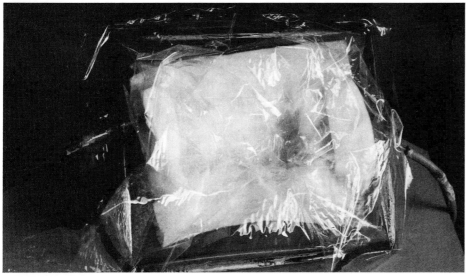

The mould with the vacuum bag in place. Note the very loose nature of the bag. This is to prevent restriction

The component is shown here under vacuum, ready for the cure

RIGHT A laminated drilling jig, which is used to ensure the accurate positioning of drilled holes

BELOW Here the component is shown in the jig and holes are being drilled

BELOW RIGHT The completed component

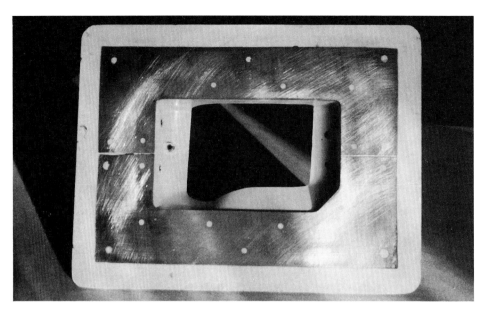

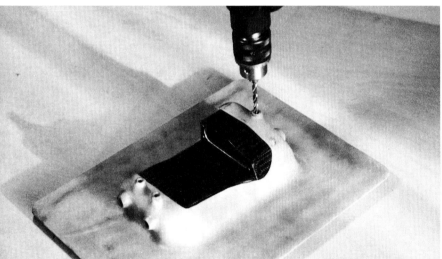

tape can be used to join sheets of vacuum-bag material. This means that there is no limit to the size of a flat vacuum bag, and tailored bags can be made by joining shaped panels of material together.

It is very important to ensure that there are no small folds in the bag material where it is sealed down, as these will produce vacuum leaks that can be difficult to find when you are trying to pull vacuum.

The bag will require two take-offs; one for a vacuum pump and the other for a vacuum gauge. These take-offs can be in the form of specially-made connectors, each having a round, two-piece base with a seal between. A hole is cut in the bag and the take-off fitted so that its split base sandwiches the vacuum-bag material.

A purpose-made take-off, or connector, usually has a non-return, or shut-off, valve and a snap-connected hose. This means that the vacuum pipe can be disconnected while maintaining the vacuum, which can be useful when the first stage of vacuum is applied on a bench. When every-

METHODS OF FORMING VACUUM BAGS FROM FLAT SHEET

A

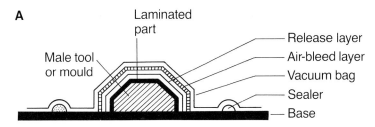

Laminated part

Male tool or mould

Release layer
Air-bleed layer
Vacuum bag
Sealer
Base

B

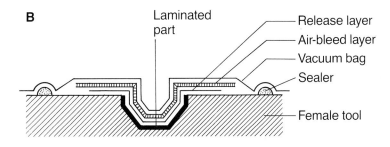

Laminated part

Release layer
Air-bleed layer
Vacuum bag
Sealer
Female tool

C

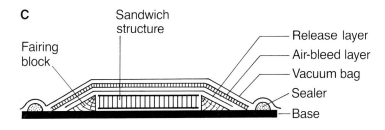

Sandwich structure

Fairing block

Release layer
Air-bleed layer
Vacuum bag
Sealer
Base

D

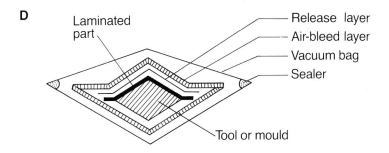

Laminated part

Release layer
Air-bleed layer
Vacuum bag
Sealer
Tool or mould

A This shows the tool and component parts to be held under vacuum on some form of solid base

B The same method as shown above, but using a female mould or tool

C This is a flat component or laminate held under vacuum on a base plate. Note the use of fairing blocks. This is to prevent the vacuum bag pulling tight over the edges of the component, which prevents excess edge pressure and protects the vacuum bag

D Here the tool and lay-up have been placed inside the vacuum bag. This is a very simple method if the tool is of a suitable size or shape

All the methods shown here are based on the use of materials described in the text

METHODS OF VACUUM TAKE-OFF

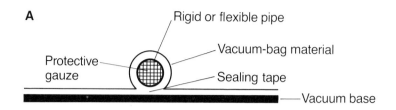

A   Rigid or flexible pipe

Protective   Vacuum-bag material
gauze

                                     Sealing tape

                                     Vacuum base

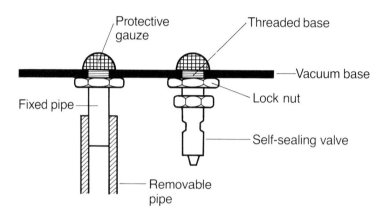

Protective   Threaded base
gauze

                         Vacuum base

Fixed pipe   Lock nut

                         Self-sealing valve

Removable
pipe

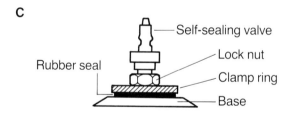

C   Self-sealing valve

                         Lock nut

Rubber seal   Clamp ring

                         Base

A This is a simple, cheap method of placing a tube directly into the edge of the vacuum bag, using vacuum-bag sealing tape. Some form of gauze or fabric should be placed over the end of the pipe to prevent it being blanked off and to maintain an air-bleed passage

B These two versions are more permanent types fixed into a base. One has a self-sealing valve for use with pre-made hoses and matching connections. The other takes a simple rubber pipe. Self-sealing valves allow the vacuum to be maintained while an assembly is transferred from bench to oven

C This type of vacuum take-off is for use in any form of flexible vacuum-bag material. It is fitted by making a hole in the material, placing the base on the inside of the vacuum bag and clamping the material between the seal and the valve body

thing is sealed and ready, the pipes can be disconnected to allow the mould to be transported to the oven.

The connection of a vacuum gauge to the second take-off allows the level of vacuum to be monitored throughout the cure.

In many cases, however, the vacuum-pump and gauge take-offs can be made with simple tubing. The tubing enters the bag via the bag seal at the mould flange. To ensure continuity of the seal, a length of sealing tape is placed round the pipe and pressed on to the sealer at the mould flange. Then the bag material is made to follow the contour of the pipe in a similar fashion to putting in a tuck.

To prevent the bag sealing over the open end of the vacuum pipe, some form of air-bleed material, such as that used to cover the lay-up, is folded several times to form a tongue-like extension to the pipe. This extension is placed so that it overlaps the bleed layer covering the lay-up, ensuring an open passage for the air being extracted.

One very important point to remember is that any tubing used for this purpose must be capable of withstanding the cure temperature. If special hoses made to fit the snap connectors are to be used, they will usually be high-temperature-resistant. If plain pipe is to be used, it is advisable to choose silicone, as this will withstand most resin cure temperatures.

With the lay-up under vacuum, check again for leaks and make sure that the vacuum bag is not bridging any point. If all is well, the assembly will be ready for curing.

The previously-described thermocouple wire should be connected to the electronic thermometer; the vacuum pump switched on, with an acceptable vacuum level achieved; and the oven turned on so that heat-up can begin.

Some ovens will have programmable temperature control, and others will also have autographic recording. These features may be essential when manufacturing parts for the aerospace industry, but many ovens

This is a typical vacuum pump used for forming pre-preg or wet lay-up consolidation.

RUBBER VACUUM BAGS

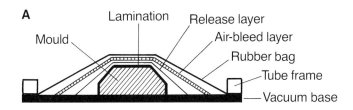

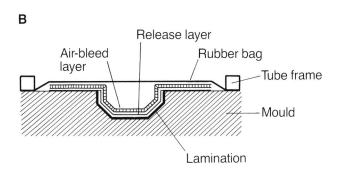

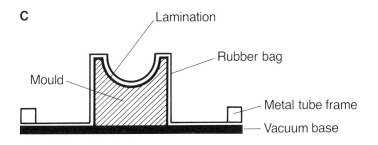

A The rubber sheet is attached to a tubular metal frame forming a diaphragm. This is placed over the mould and the frame clamped to the vacuum base. Under vacuum, the rubber stretches to the component's shape
B This method is similar to the one above, but the rubber stretches to the shape of a female mould
C This method is also similar, but the vacuum bag is tailored to the mould shape. This is used when the mould is of complex shape. These types of bag are professionally made
Rubber vacuum bags are ideal where many mouldings are needed or when made to fit a general vacuum base. This prevents the need to make disposable bags for each moulding

ABOVE A vertical oven used for composite material cures, but ovens can be of any size or shape. Even heat distribution is very important, as is good insulation

ABOVE RIGHT A large, curved component under vacuum and about to be put into an autoclave for the cure cycle

will be operated manually, assisted by a simple thermostat.

Using the same type of mould and lay-up, the cure can be carried out in an autoclave. The difference between this method and an oven cure is that the autoclave will provide a much higher pressure, which can be used to consolidate very thick laminates or force pre-preg lay-ups into tight corners and shapes. In some cases, the higher pressure serves to force out excess resin when a large number of pre-preg layers is used. Autoclaves are expensive to purchase and run, but most composite work is possible using the oven and vacuum method.

The manufacturer's technical data will give cure requirements for the chosen pre-preg. This will include minimum and maximum temperature during the cure. In some cases, the resin type, or the type of lamination, will require a specific heat-up rate, that is a certain number of degrees per minute up to cure temperature.

When the assembly has passed through the specified cure cycle, the heat supply should be turned off, but vacuum maintained until the temperature has dropped to 70°C or lower.

If the vacuum bag is removed carefully, it may be retained for further use. This should only be in, or on, the same mould, as the material tends to harden a little with use.

Component removal should be quite straightforward. The first step is to remove any excess resin that may have flowed out over any joins in the mould. With the connecting bolts, if used, removed, the joining flanges may be gently prised apart and the mould lifted off the component.

Where the component is large, or deep, in shape, it is advisable to use a rubber mallet to give firm, but controlled, blows over the mould's outer surface. This produces shock waves which will, in most cases, be of considerable assistance in separating the component from the mould.

On very large moulds, air connectors are built into the surface, allowing connection of a compressed-air line. This is used to blow air between the mould face and component, again assisting in the removal of the component.

Once the laminated pre-preg component has been removed from the mould, all that remains is to trim and finish it. This usually consists of removing flash lines, that is the lines produced by the joins in the mould, and the trimming of excess material from around the component's edges. Gel-coat material, or some form of filler, can be used to fill any surface indentations or holes.

The flash lines and any other minor blemishes can be removed by using wet-or-dry papers, the final finish being achieved with cutting or polishing compound, such as that used to polish car paint. If the component is to be painted, care should be taken not to use polishing compounds based on wax.

The finished component can be primed and painted by most normal processes. Carbon-fibre components are often left as polished or, in some cases, have some form of clear lacquer applied to enhance their appearance.

The curved honeycomb sandwich structure after removal from the bonding tool

Laminating conclusion

Laminating in all forms requires a high degree of common sense, which is why the end result can be achieved by different routes—a component can meet the required standard when made by differing methods and with different materials. Design and cost are the main deciding factors, but other considerations, such as available equipment, etc, must also be taken into account.

Composite technology has produced a wide range of available materials from many manufacturers. This, in turn, had led to many different processes and techniques. The text of this book is aimed at giving an insight into the possible range of materials and processing requirements and techniques, which is essential if design in composite materials is to be part of the project.

5 Fabrication by cut-and-fold

TOP RIGHT   This and the following series of photographs show the most widely used forms of routing cutters on composite structures. This pineapple-type cutter can be used on a wide range of materials, but is ideal on sandwich panels that have very fibrous skins, such as multi-layer UD pre-preg. It gives best results when run at high speed

CENTRE RIGHT   Normal fluted cutter, which is mainly used on solid laminates and sandwich panels. It can be used to cut part way through the panel thickness

RIGHT   This is a fluted cutter, but it has a roller bearing of the same size centred on the bottom end. Using this bearing as a guide against a template, as shown, it can be used to trim composite panels or to profile shaped panel sections

Composite component manufacture has been dealt with from the laminating and moulding point of view, but there is another method of utilizing sandwich structures that are supplied as purpose-made, or off-the-shelf, pre-made, flat panels. This extremely useful and widely-used method is the cut-and-fold technique.

If one skin of a sandwich panel is cut through and some material removed, this has the effect of weakening the structure, allowing the panel to be bent at that point. If a suitable adhesive is put into the cut area and the panel bent and held in position until the adhesive has cured, the bend will remain set with considerable strength. If necessary, the joint strength can be improved by bonding a covering strip over the cut area. A high percentage of the original skin performance can be maintained in this way.

The interesting point is that by using the formula $2\pi t\dfrac{x}{360}$, where t equals panel thickness and x equals required bend angle, it is a simple matter to calculate the amount of material to remove to produce any required bend angle from any reasonable panel thickness.

Using the cut-and-fold method, a very wide range of component shapes can be produced. This range can be extended to include curves and large- or small-radius bends. These are achieved by making a series of closely-spaced cuts, a small circular or slitting saw being ideal for this. Even tubes and pipes can be produced from flat panels in this manner, as can aerofoil shapes. The possibilities are almost endless.

The great advantage of this method of fabrication is that due to the area between the skin cuts being a structural section that does not bend, the required shape is almost self-jigging. Clamps alone, or even sticky tape, are sufficient to produce many shapes.

The most widely used adhesive systems employed for this type of construction come from the epoxy range. In most cases, they are of the right consistency for the application and capable of achieving a high level of performance.

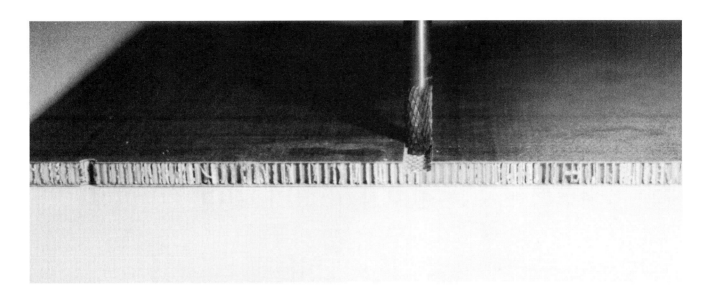

This close-up shows cut-and-fold, metal-skinned honeycomb building panels during early assembly

Composite honeycomb sandwich structures have been utilized to great effect by the building industry to stabilize cladding panels. Many types of facing skin can be used for this type of exterior or interior panelling. Shown here is an exterior-clad building

Cut-and-fold can be utilized on many types of sandwich structure. With honeycomb as a core material, reasonable strength is achieved by the fact that adhesive put into the open areas of the cut bonds the cells of the honeycomb together. This situation is enhanced by the fact that the act of folding closes up the cells at that point. This results in an increase in density, hence the immediate strength level.

As previously mentioned, where convenient or considered necessary, a covering strip bonded over the closed joint will improve the skin continuity, providing added strength.

Where foams are used as core materials, the need to use a covering strip becomes much more important. This is because the foam strength is only as good as the cellular strength, that is the load required to break the bubbles that make up the foam. Structural foams are much better in this respect, but will not perform as well as the honeycomb. Therefore, covering strips are more important, and are essential with low-density or insulation-type foams.

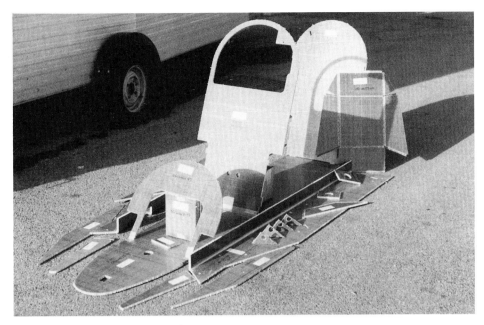

Pre-cut honeycomb sandwich shapes form the basis of the CFM Shadow fuselage. Shown here are component parts prior to fabrication

The fuselage footwell is fabricated from honeycomb sandwich by the cut-and-fold method

The first stage of fabrication. Note the simplicity of assembly

TOP The main fuselage frame is seen here after the first stage of bonding

ABOVE One stage further in the fabrication of the fuselage shows the addition of the wing centre mounting frames

LEFT The wing structure consists of ribs made from profiled styrofoam, encased by wet lay-up glass fibre and built on to a wooden box-type main spar and leading edge

This photograph shows the method of making an ultra-light fuel tank for a microlight aircraft. The material is aluminium honeycomb, faced with glass fibre pre-preg to form a sandwich structure. The panel sections are bonded together using two-part epoxy adhesive

Here is the complete fuselage ready to fly

The very successful CFM Shadow in flight. At the time of writing, over 90 of this type of aircraft have been produced

This and the following photographs show how the cut-and-fold method of fabrication is utilized to manufacture aircraft overhead luggage bins. As these bins are made in large numbers, the blanks are shaped by CNC programme routing. One such batch is shown here

Here is the routed shape. Note the close cuts to form a large-radius curve

This photograph shows a blank in the assembly jig. This holds the component in an accurate shape while the adhesive cures. In most cases, two-part epoxy is used

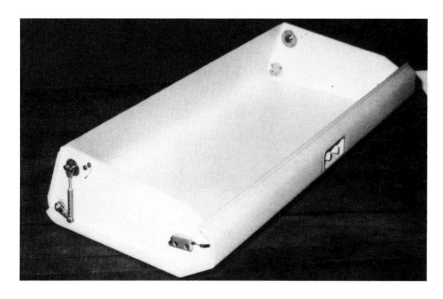

The completed luggage bin
ready for fitting into an aircraft

This form of fabrication has found a wide use in many industries, and in many cases has been put on a production-line basis to generate volume output. Once the shape required to produce the component, however simple or complicated, has been worked out, the flat panels can be cut using almost any practical method, the most widely-used being some form of hand-held or automatic router. Where a large number of parts, or extreme accuracy, is required, CNC machinery is ideal. As previously mentioned, a saw of some form can be used for very narrow cuts.

This form of fabrication has been used for the manufacture of aircraft components, such as overhead racks, galleys, etc and, in some cases, air-frame components. Race-car chassis have been made using this method, as have motorcycle chassis, enclosures for electronics, box beams for various structural applications, and many other items. The list is almost endless, as is the potential.

The unique cut-and-fold method of construction brings the potential of one aspect of composite use to almost anyone, even if facilities are limited, as flat, pre-made sandwich panels are available from various suppliers for those who cannot, or do not wish to, produce their own.

Agriculture has also utilized modern composites by using honeycomb sandwich to fabricate the box sections that make up this ultra-light 24-metre spray boom. In steel, a boom of this size would weigh in the region of 1300 kg. This composite version weighs 350 kg.

6 Composite design

Modern composite materials and techniques have much to offer designers in many fields. A well-established user of these materials is the aircraft industry, both civil and military aircraft now utilizing composite materials in large quantities. Carbon fibre is used in many structural applications, and phenolics are used in conjunction with glass or Kevlar to produce flame-retardant cabin components.

The race-car industry is almost totally dependent on composite materials, again both structurally and for bodywork. Carbon fibre on honeycomb is now standard chassis-building practice.

Composites are also utilized in the construction of commercial vehicles, especially delivery vehicles, where the use of lightweight composite materials can increase valuable payload capacity. Passenger-carrying vehicles are using more composite materials, too, either for their fire-retardant properties or, in the case of boats and ships, as a means of saving weight. The materials are often used in vehicles and ships to simplify construction, that is light, but very stiff, panels can be produced that allow structures to be built with a minimum of framework or, to put it simply, that are self-supporting.

Many forms of composite panelling are now widely employed in the building industry, both for exterior and interior use. Often, where composite panelling is used for interiors, it will be utilized for its stability to provide a base on to which other materials may be applied for decorative purposes.

One major area where design in composite materials has taken giant steps is in the sports equipment industry, the possibilities being almost endless. Significant products include golf-club shafts, tennis and other rackets, composite bows for archery, skis (both snow and water versions), race-type rowing craft and canoes, sailboards and other sailing craft, racing power boats, and light sports aircraft and gliders.

These sports applications have utilized composite materials in positive structural situations and, therefore, would have needed a degree of structural design to produce the components in new materials to meet the required level of performance. All composite applications will need some degree of design, but for the purpose of this section of the book, it is assumed that designed components will occur where some form of structural requirement prevails.

Designing in composite to meet a specific structural performance is much more difficult if the component is being manufactured for the first time, that is when there are no previous components in conventional materials that would serve as a performance control or guideline. However, where the composite component is a direct copy of, or very similar to, an existing component in conventional materials, a bench-mark, or performance level, exists against which the performance of the new composite design can be compared.

The need, or desire, to redesign a component in composite materials can occur for various reasons; for example, to improve structural performance, to reduce component weight, to provide better fatigue performance, or to simplify the method of manufacture. There are many other reasons, too.

However, there are many cases where a new composite design will incorporate more than one of the benefits mentioned above, such as greater strength combined with lighter weight or improved fatigue life. Another important aspect is that some critical structures can have much greater strength under impact conditions, which, under the right circumstances can lead to greater safety.

A current single-seater racing-car chassis in carbon fibre and honeycomb is an excellent example of many of these composite virtues in one structure. There are many examples from the aerospace industry with similar virtues. Sports applications and many others also utilize the facility of incorporating more than one aspect of improved performance in the new design.

Although design work may still be required for non-structural or semistructural applications, such as bodywork, ducting, enclosures, etc, the term 'design', when used in this section of the book, is applied specifically to applications with structural requirements.

Some levels of design, whatever the materials used, should be undertaken by trained experts in the materials concerned, who have an understanding of the intended structure and its performance requirements.

Under normal circumstances, a multi-storey building would be designed by an architect, and a large ship by a naval architect; but in the world of composites, where there is little formal design training, the designers of major structural components have utilized their understanding of basic design requirements for conventional materials and replaced these with the relevant data for composite materials. This replacement of data is not quite as straightforward as it first sounds, for composite materials have their own specific behaviour patterns, which must be studied and understood.

Composite materials will have behaviour patterns that are totally different from conventional materials that would have normally been used for the selected application, but can have advantageous aspects as well. The designer, therefore, will utilize these advantages. This will, however, require a new design theme in view of the differing behaviour patterns.

An example of utilizing the advantages provided by a composite material is where a component that needs to be light in weight also has stiffness as an important structural requirement. With conventional materials, in most cases, it would be necessary to add more material to achieve additional stiffness, but this would produce a weight penalty. With composites, all that may be necessary to achieve the stiffness requirement is specific orientation of the fibres in a laminate, that is a larger percentage of the fibres would be placed parallel to the longitudinal axis of the required stiffness plane. This has the effect of achieving the structural performance without the addition of unwanted weight, and in some cases weight may even be reduced.

The example quoted above is one of many, and it is these advantages that must be examined and justified, that is from both the technical and cost aspects. In some industries, these composite advantages have been exploited to the extent that it would be very difficult, if not impossible, to return to the use of conventional materials.

If the composite design to be undertaken is a replacement component or structure, then some form of performance level will have been set by the original component. Utilizing the performance data for the available composite materials, it will be possible to design to meet, or better, the standard set. It may, of course, be imperative that a higher structural performance is achieved, which may be the reason for the use of composite materials.

Where the component or structure has to be of a similar physical layout or shape to the original in conventional materials, the designer has a good basis on which to design the composite replacement.

Manufacturer's technical data will give performance levels for the available range of composite materials. From this data the designer will select the appropriate material and method to produce a composite component of similar physical proportions to the original, with equal or, in most cases, much improved performance levels. For example, sheets or sections of aluminium will have known performance levels for each specific type. This standard data will be used by the designer to achieve a performance requirement from a component or structure manufactured from the selected aluminium. If the component was a sandwich structure with aluminium skins, then composite skins would replace the aluminium ones on the same basis, as described above.

The same basic principle would apply when creating a similar physical shape. Whatever the shape of the original, if there is a performance requirement on the proposed component, and the performance specification of the conventional material used for the original component is known, the designer can readily substitute the selected composite materials. He will, of course, have to consider the processing method for the composite materials, which is an important factor.

So far, these outline notes on composite design have been limited to the production of a composite replacement, of similar physical shape, for something that has been manufactured in conventional materials. However, the production of a direct, or almost direct, copy of a component in composite is a fairly rare situation, particularly when the component is of a structural nature. Therefore, if full advantage is to be taken of the composite's potential, designing the replacement will be much more difficult. This is due to the probability of the new design having an entirely different configuration in terms of shape and layout. The complication is compounded by the fact that there are so many composite materials and methods of use to be considered before the designer arrives at the new component's configuration.

If there are no performance details for an existing component that is to be replaced by one made of a composite material, in many cases the replacement is made by 'hit-or-miss' methods. The existing component will still prove useful, however, since its make-up will give a good performance test, such as for stiffness, impact resistance, or ultimate strength, can be carried out to set a level for the new design.

Where the new design is also the first component or structure made for the planned application, it is important, of course, to know what the performance requirement is before beginning to design the composite component.

If it is not possible to access the performance requirement for the new design, then one possible starting point is to visualize the component in a conventional material, such as steel or aluminium. This will give some idea of performance requirement, although, unless tests are carried out, this method cannot be quantified. Under these circumstances, the new design should have some built-in safety by being over-engineered—not a bad policy with the use of totally new materials and concepts.

The approach to designing in composites will depend on many aspects, particularly the skill of the designer. Some will be capable of utilizing composites even in primary structures with safety and in many cases, safety levels will improve; others will be capable of utilizing components made from conventional materials as bench-marks from which to judge the performance of the composite replacements. Where the nature of the structure allows, one design method that may be adopted is to construct the part and, if it fails, to make it stronger. Another is to work in reverse; over-engineer, then cut back to the required or acceptable level.

The latter methods of approach to design should not be taken too lightly. Adopting the 'if it breaks, make it stronger' method is only an extension of evaluation testing; the component itself simply becomes the test-piece. Provided close note is taken during the design and manufacture of components or structures in this manner, useful design and material information can be gathered that will be invaluable in further development or design situations. This also serves to give the designer an intimate knowledge of composites and their capabilities, as well as helping to raise confidence levels.

Design and material comparisons

The comparison between composite and conventional material performances is an excellent introduction to understanding composite performance potentials. When beginning to design in composites this potential should be utilized. However, the physical shape, or layout, of any previous component in conventional materials should not, in most cases, be considered as a pattern for the new composite design.

Composite materials may have the potential to vastly improve on the performance of an existing component or structure, but the physical shape or layout may have to be very different to achieve the structural improvement. This is why it is important to consider composites as a completely new material range and to design for their use from the beginning.

Although, in some circumstances, composite materials can be made into components of similar shape to conventional materials with, in some cases, improved performance, this situation can be misleading. For example, it is possible to produce carbon-fibre tubes that can display great advantages over steel or aluminium tubes, when tested as tubes. However, it would be wrong to design any form of frame—for a car, motorcycle, aircraft or any other application—based on space-frame technology, but using carbon-fibre tubes. This does not apply to the use of carbon-fibre tubing as a single item, such as some form of spar or shaft, where the composite can often out-perform other materials and also be lighter.

Although steel tubes have been used very successfully for space-frame structures for many years, and great effort has been made by the use of high-grade steels, etc to optimize the overall performance of the structure, there are limiting factors. These include reaching very high levels of bending and torsional stiffness.

The basic layout of a space frame usually consists of main longitudinal members with spacer members. The longitudinal members are supported by the cross-members when subjected to bending and twisting forces. Triangulation of the cross-members optimizes this support by arranging some cross-members so that they are in tension, while others are in compression. However, it is not practical to provide total support to any of the frame members and, therefore, there are limitations with this type of structure. In space-frame design added strength means added weight.

The weakness of a space-frame is its unsupported areas of tubing, which allow bending or twisting to take place under the appropriate loading. This problem is overcome on larger structures, such as bridges, etc, by the use of larger tubes or girders but, in these cases, there is no weight penalty.

One major design advance that was to overcome many space-frame problems was the stressed-skin monocoque.

Stressed-skin structures were originally utilized by the aerospace industry, but were taken up by the motor racing designers who saw to it that the single-skin monocoque became widely used for sportscars and single-seaters. Chassis layout, using this method of construction, would vary widely from car to car and from designer to designer. However, the basic monocoque principle consisted of a series of longitudinal torsion boxes spaced by a floor and various bulkheads.

In most cases, the torsion boxes were formed from aluminium sheet although, to a limited extent, steel sheet was used. They would have diaphragms, or formers, of the same material placed inside to stabilize the structure. The bulkheads would either be machined castings or, in many cases, two skins, again with spacers or formers between them. The complete structure was riveted together, a method long used in the aerospace industry. Similar principles were applicable to single- or two-seater monocoques.

This type of chassis, or monocoque, was to show many major structural improvements; a significant technical advance was that it was lighter and stiffer than a space-frame in both bending and torsional planes.

Increased stiffness with lighter weight was achieved, in the main, because this form of structure was able to utilize a higher percentage of the selected material's performance.

Unlike the space-frame, where the unsupported areas of tube give rise to bending, a box formed from sheet material, such as the torsion boxes of a monocoque, has no unsupported areas. The side-members of the box in the vertical plane carry the bending loads. The top and bottom of the box, and any bulkheads or diaphragms placed inside, act as spacers, or stabilizers, to retain the true box dimensions while under load.

Torsional stiffness in a stressed-skin monocoque is achieved by the overall shape or layout and the way in which the component parts are joined together. For example, with a wide monocoque, such as a two-seater, apart from the performance of the individual side box-members in resisting the bending loads, the way in which they are connected, by the bulkheads and floor, will, to a great extent, control the overall torsional stiffness.

In the case of a narrow monocoque, such as for a single-seater, where there are no large torsion boxes, the sides, bottom and top must be constructed to resist both bending and torsional loads. In most cases, this was achieved by incorporating a double-skin arrangement wherever possible. For example, the outer skin of the monocoque would have other panels, such as cockpit lining panels, bulkheads, etc, all connected by diaphragms or stabilizers; in effect, they would form a long, thin torsion box.

The stressed-skin monocoque became a standard method of race-car construction, but it did have its drawbacks. One was the necessity of fitting highly-stressed mounting points for the engine, suspension, etc. This was achieved by designing suitable load-spreader mountings, the base of each having sufficient area to distribute the point loads into the monocoque skin to which it was attached. In some cases, machined bulkheads would carry some loads. This type of monocoque was generally more expensive to manufacture than a space-frame but, more importantly, it was much more difficult to repair.

As previously stated, the stressed-skin monocoque was a great advance on the tubular space-frame in many ways, but it still had one major drawback, and that was the tendency for the skins to buckle under load. More diaphragms and bulkheads would provide an improvement, as would increases in skin thickness, but these were limiting from both the practical and weight aspects.

To combat the skin buckling problem, one form of composite was utilized in aluminium-skinned monocoques, and that was honeycomb.

The overall box form of the monocoque was retained, but each wall of the box, or boxes, consisted of a sandwich structure of honeycomb between aluminium sheets. The performance of this sandwich structure was predetermined by selection of the density and type of honeycomb, together with the thickness and specification of the skin material.

The monocoque's overall performance was greatly improved by the fact that the monocoque walls were a structure themselves, that is they were, in effect double-skinned with honeycomb cores. The honeycomb supported the skins over a large percentage of the surface area, resulting in a structure with a much greater resistance to buckling.

Another advantage of this type of structure was the facility for fitting hardpoints, that is mounting points for bolt-on parts. Due to the monocoque walls being double-skinned, and both skins being supported over a large percentage of their surface area, inserts could be used. These could consist of a block of aluminium, or some other suitable material, cut to the required size and put into the honeycomb sandwich when it was being made. Subsequently, the insert was drilled for the component at some suitable stage of the monocoque's construction.

Another method of installing inserts consisted of putting them in as a later operation, after the honeycomb sandwich, or the monocoque, had been completed. These could be of a type known as potted inserts, or single- or two-part, surface-mounted inserts.

Potting inserts requires a hole to be bored in the appropriate position, the hole matching the widest diameter of a cotton-reel-shaped insert. The insert is positioned in the hole and a resin, specially formulated for the purpose, is injected through a small hole in the insert's flange, filling the waisted centre-section of the insert, together with the surrounding honeycomb cells. Another small hole in the opposite side of the same flange allows excess resin to escape and acts as an indicator that the internal cavity is full. The two-part, adhesive-type potting compound is then cured at room temperature, or slightly higher.

The surface-mounted insert consists of a round rod that has been turned to leave a thin disc-like flange at the end, usually about twice the diameter of the insert body. In some cases, this type of insert is made as a two-piece unit, that is it has a flange at each end and is split in the middle. Sometimes, one piece is made so that it is an interference fit in the other to aid installation.

When fitting a surface-mounted insert, it is necessary to drill a normal, parallel-sided hole through the sandwich panel, matching the size of the

RIGHT Some typical honeycomb sandwich-panel finishing methods, including joints, edges and inserts

Typical flat panel edging methods

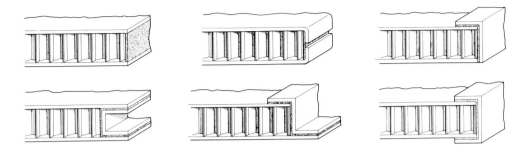

Typical flat panel joints and corners

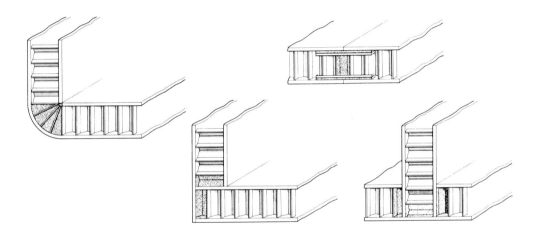

Typical fastening methods

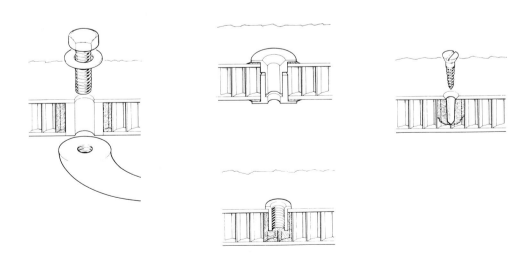

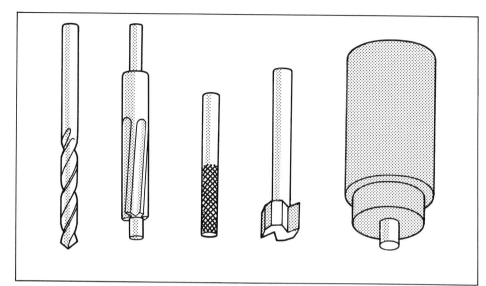

A selection of tools for fabricating components from pre-made panels. They are suitable for use with a hand or fixed router

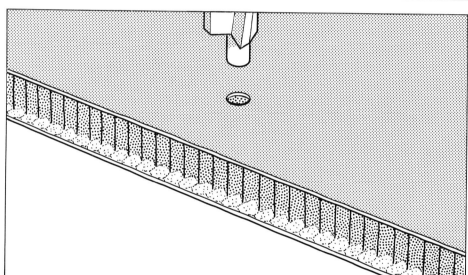

Pilot hole being drilled for an insert

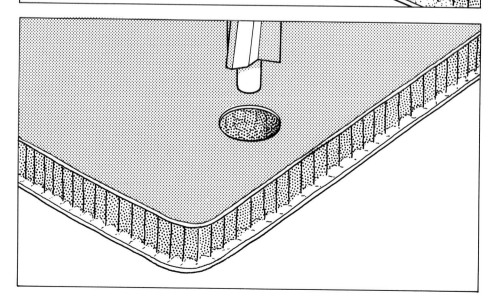

Routing cutter using pilot hole

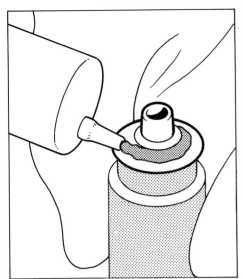
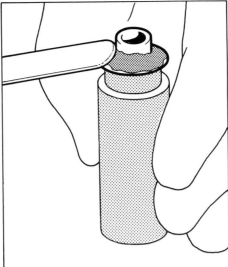

Adhesive being applied to both sides of a two-piece insert

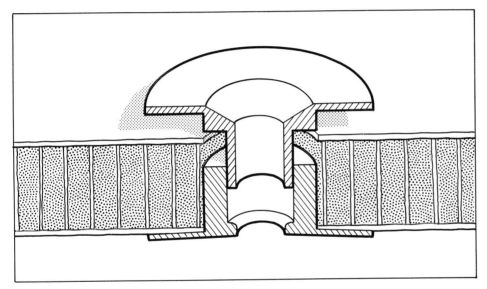

A typical two-piece insert shown partly installed

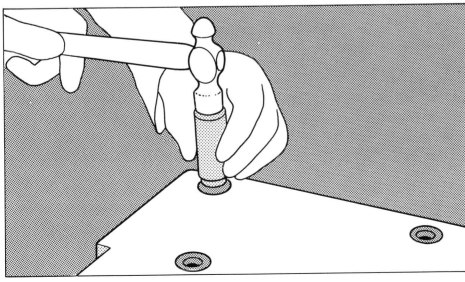

A sharp blow with a hammer will force the two parts together, and their interference fit will hold them in place while the adhesive sets

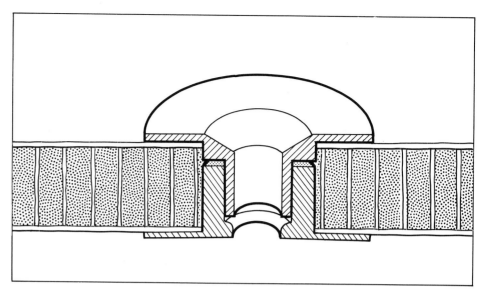

The insert in place

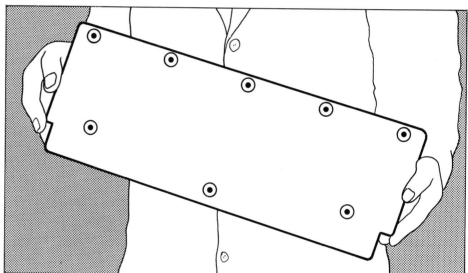

A typical panel designed to be fixed by the use of two-piece inserts

insert's body. Then two-part epoxy adhesive is applied to the underside of the flange, or flanges, and the insert is pushed into the panel.

In the case of the one-piece, or single-sided, type, some form of light pressure is applied while the adhesive is cured at room temperature or higher. This pressure can be applied by a clamp bolt or similar device.

In the case of the two-part insert, the pieces are put into the sandwich panel from each side and pressed together, the interference fit holding them while the adhesive cure takes place.

The single-sided type of insert is normally used where the sandwich panel is to be secured to something else. However, where the sandwich panel is freestanding and another component is to be attached to it, the two-piece variety is the most suitable type.

These types of insert work by distributing the input loads into the sandwich structure's skins. The size of the flange will determine, to a great extent, the level of the insert's performance. Both types, and a large selec-

ABOVE An early F1 race-car chassis made by the cut-and-fold technique from pre-made, aluminium-skinned, aluminium honeycomb panels

BELOW LEFT Another early race-car chassis made by cut-and-fold from pre-made, flat panels, but utilizing carbon fibre as the panel skins

BELOW RIGHT A much later F1 chassis made by moulding carbon fibre pre-preg on to a honeycomb core. The almost standard method by which current chassis are made

tion of variants, are commercially available, although some users manufacture their own.

Monocoque construction, using honeycomb in a sandwich structure, can be carried out by two main methods. One is to preform the aluminium skins, which are then bonded together, using a structural adhesive, in a mould or jig. This method allows the use of the internal type of hardpoint or insert.

The other method of monocoque construction using honeycomb sandwich is to employ pre-made flat panels of the selected sandwich thickness. These can be formed into the required shapes by utilizing the cut-and-fold method of construction, as described previously.

One limiting factor can be the skin material. For example, glass-fibre skins lend themselves to this form of manufacture, but some carbon-fibre types are too stiff and brittle. However, the fibre type and weave style may make the bending possible. Kevlar works very well for cut-and-fold. Metals, such as steel and aluminium, are ideal for use as skin materials when utilizing the cut-and-fold method of manufacture.

The use of honeycomb to stabilize the skins of a sandwich for the manufacture of many structural components, especially racing-car chassis or monocoques, became a standard method of improving the structural performance. In addition, employing honeycomb sandwich was becoming the standard method of meeting structural requirements in other industries, including aerospace applications.

Modern composite materials have enabled designers to take the performance levels of honeycomb sandwich structures to a much higher level.

The main structural requirements from a sandwich structure are dependent on the performance of the skin materials. It would, of course, be possible to improve the performance of most sandwich structures by a marked increase in skin thickness, or by using steel in place of aluminium. However, this type of change would impose a severe weight penalty, and in most cases where honeycomb sandwich is being utilized, it is to produce high-performance, but light, structures.

There are some exceptions where weight is not important and honeycomb is being used for stability—types of surface table, etc. These are areas where the skin can be almost anything, provided the required performance is achieved.

Because it is possible, with the aid of modern composite materials—carbon fibre in particular—to achieve a higher skin performance without an increase in weight, the use of honeycomb sandwich has been taken to even higher performance levels.

There are many applications for this type of structure, but the designers of racing-car chassis, or monocoques, and now motorcycles, are taking full advantage of these materials. It is interesting to note that several race-car formulae, including Formula One, are totally dependent on this form of structure.

Exceptions are cars for the CART series in the USA, and some others, where the chassis, by regulation, has to have a deformable structure. In most cases, this results in a monocoque made in two main pieces. The top half will be manufactured as a composite sandwich structure, often carbon fibre on honeycomb. Usually, the lower half will also consist of honeycomb sandwich, comprising aluminium skins on aluminium honeycomb. This lower half is stiff, but the malleability of the aluminium produces a structure that will, in a serious accident, deform and not fracture.

The differing regulations that produce designs and structures which perform in a similar fashion when being used as intended, but react in a totally different manner when crashed, serve to illustrate the versatility of composite materials, even under structural conditions.

Composite versatility can be taken even further and used primarily to provide a safety aid. The incorporation of a fail-safe, in the form of Kevlar being used as part of a laminate, has already been mentioned. Kevlar is also used in several forms as a prime form of ballistic protection in bulletproof clothing, and body armour, etc. However, such highly-specialized technology is not a subject for this book, but it does illustrate the potential of composite materials.

Those intending to carry out a design based on the use of composites, but with no previous experience of these materials, should first make an effort to understand the potential performances of each material type, and this should include the processing requirements. Most important, however, is an understanding of the way in which composites can have, in some cases, a mechanically superior structural performance, although in other respects, their behaviour may be totally different to conventional materials. For example, if loaded to destruction, the mode, or type, of failure may be totally different, which can be a major consideration.

When an aluminium or steel structure is loaded beyond its elastic limit, permanent deformation takes place in varying degrees. However, if the same component is designed around the use of carbon fibre, it may be able to take a greater load. Unfortunately, with carbon fibre having little or no elastic limit, when failure occurs it will be almost total. This is the reason for the use of Kevlar in some structures to act as a flexible element preventing total fragmentation.

One very important aspect in favour of composite structures is their renowned fatigue resistance.

The performance of any new design is dependent on the performance of the individual materials from which it is to be manufactured.

Failure mode and fatigue have been mentioned. The next stage is to consider the aspects that control, to a great degree, the ultimate overall performance. These are density, strength and modulus. Density controls, or determines, the component or structure weight; strength and modulus, the mechanical performance.

Density is easily explained as weight per unit volume; strength is the load required to break, or cause to fail, any specific cross-section of the material under study, and specific strength is the load required to break a material, or cause it to fail, but is related to a specified weight and not the material cross-section. Specific strength levels are arrived at by divid-

FIBRE DIRECTIONS TO MEET TUBE OR PIPE PERFORMANCE REQUIREMENTS

A Bending

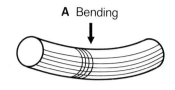

B Hoop

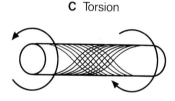

C Torsion

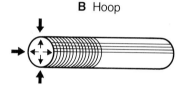

A To produce tubes with longitudinal stiffness, a much larger percentage of fibres should be placed along the tube. It is very important to have a small percentage placed around the tube; the percentages should be in the form of complete fibre layers
B To produce good hoop strength, that is resistance to internal or external pressure, the larger percentage of fibres should be placed round the tube, with a smaller percentage along the tube. These percentages should be in the form of complete fibre layers
C Where torsional strength is the important requirement, the fibres should be placed at ± 45 degrees

ing the material strength by its density. The resultant information is of particular interest to the designer.

Modulus is the measure of a material's stiffness but, unfortunately, is not a single measure of material performance. For example, there is tensile modulus (*tensile load ÷ tensile strain*); shear modulus (*shear stress ÷ shear strain*); modulus of elasticity, Young's Modulus (*stress ÷ strain*); and specific modulus (*Young's Modulus ÷ density*).

Young's and specific moduli are of prime importance. They are most widely used by designers in composite materials, especially in primary structural applications, such as chassis, spars, monocoques, frames etc.

Designing in any material, but particularly composites, is not simply a matter of utilizing a single performance from that material, that is its strength, modulus, etc. It may be essential to consider several aspects of the selected material's performance to achieve the required mechanical performance.

For example, ultra-high-modulus carbon fibre may produce the required component stiffness with a very small cross-sectional area, but the lower specific strength of this type of carbon fibre may make it unsuitable for another reason, such as poor impact resistance. This could be overcome by the use of a lower-modulus carbon fibre with a higher specific strength. The required stiffness would be achieved by using a little more material which, in turn, would produce an increased cross-sectional area.

The figures shown in the chart below give an indication of material comparison. The composite figures represent unidirectional fibre with an epoxy matrix resin, and for the purpose of the comparison, the figures are for the materials loaded in tension.

	Alloy	Steel	Kevlar	Carbon	High Mod Carbon	Ultra High Mod Carbon
Specific modulus	1.2	1.2	2	3.8	5.6	8.2
Specific strength	0.8	1.5	4	4.3	2.6	1.5

It must be noted that the composite elements in the chart are based on unidirectional fibres, and in an actual component a proportion of these, possibly up to 50 per cent, would lie in a direction other than the direction of stress. This is an important point that must be taken into account when designing, so that sufficient material is placed in position to cope with input stress. This is why it is advantageous to know how the proposed structure or component is to be stressed.

It can be seen from the material comparisons that low-density materials, such as the composites, will produce a larger cross-sectional area for the same weight, and this factor can be utilized to achieve great stiffness. For example, if steel was replaced by the same weight of the lowest specific-modulus carbon fibre, the stiffness would be over three times greater. This means that improvement in flexural stiffness can be achieved through both cross-sectional stiffness and the material's specific properties.

If, however, the cross-section has a size limitation, the sectional advantage can be lost; for example, in the case of rods or small-diameter pipes, where the limitation of material volume prevents the use of low-density, but high-specific-modulus materials, such as carbon fibre. Also, the fibres laying on and adjacent to the neutral axis carry little, or none, of the bending stress and, therefore, offer nothing to the flexural stiffness.

The point regarding the neutral axis applies, of course, to any section during bending. If a rod or bar has sufficient bending stress applied to cause deflection, the material on the outside of the bend is put in tension, while the material on the inside of the bend is in compression. Therefore, the transition point between tension and compression does not contribute to either mode of stress, adding little or nothing to the mechanical performance. Consequently, the designer must include sufficient material in these areas to achieve the required structural performance. This point illustrates the versatility of composites as structural materials.

Pipes and tubes for many applications utilize composite materials. The advantages, apart from very low weight, are that any size or shape can be manufactured, and that fibre orientation allows the designer to utilize the materials to achieve the required performance from the finished pipe.

The choice of materials for pipe or tube manufacture will depend on the usual parameters; performance requirement, cost, available equipment, etc. Most of these points will be answered automatically, but the way in which the selected materials are utilized may not be so obvious.

Tubes that are to be stiff to resist bending must have most of the fibres running at o degrees, that is lengthwise along the pipe. The remainder of the fibre content should run at ±45 degrees or 90 degrees. These cross-fibres hold the main fibres in place and give the component some strength other than bending resistance alone.

Tubes that need hoop strength, to resist direct external clamping or internal pressure, will have most of the fibres at 90 degrees, that is round the pipe. The remainder of the fibre content will be at o degrees, (lengthwise) or at ±45 degrees.

Tubes to meet torsional requirements, such as drive shafts, etc, will have all the fibres in a helix at +45 degrees/−45 degrees.

The description of the fibre orientation for tube manufacture is intended as a guide only. There may be situations where the application demands a performance in more than one of the described modes. In that situation a more complex make-up of fibre orientation will be necessary, but this, and the type of composite material to be used, will have to be designed in, or arrived at, by sample testing.

If the first new design in composite materials is a direct replacement for an existing structure in conventional materials, such as wood or metal, then use relative modulus and strength data to arrive at a starting point for a structural performance level. If no data is available for the conventional materials to be replaced, or if the structure is complex, a simple, static deflection test would give a good indication.

For a simple deflection test, it is neccessary to select a set sample, or

The amount of fibre, the direction percentages and the resultant tube wall thickness are points that must be arrived at to meet the tube's specific needs from all performance aspects

TYPES OF LOAD

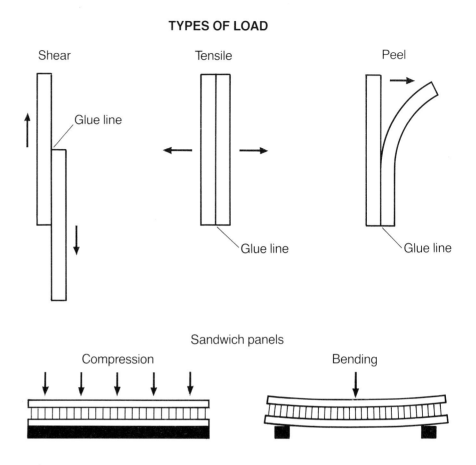

The type of load must be considered when selecting the adhesive system. Adhesives with very high shear strength will not be as good in peel and vice versa. There are adhesives that have reasonable performance for all types of load. In the case of sandwich panels, the core material must be considered in addition to the adhesive from points such as compressive and core shear performance

specimen, size; 10 × 4 in. is often used, but provided the same size is used throughout the tests, a specimen convenient in size will provide an indication of material comparison. Each specimen is supported a short distance in from each end, and is very important to ensure that the supports are always in exactly the same place. The specimen is then loaded by placing a static weight on its centre. A dial gauge set up under the centre of the specimen will show the amount of deflection.

The deflection test will give a good indication of differing materials' performances. Also, very important when using composite materials, it will serve as an excellent check on any theoretical specimen design, or as a stage-by-stage test on composite samples until the required performance level has been achieved.

Where available, test equipment can be utilized to a far greater extent to compare materials or test a stage-by-stage build-up. However, the tests can be more comprehensive, that is they can check differing modes, such as shear strength, tensile strength, or peel strength. Longer-term testing can be carried out on fatigue or environmental performance.

On highly-complex or primary structural components, where it is deemed necessary and is warranted from a cost aspect, a full stress analysis can be carried out. This is only viable, however, if carried out by persons experienced in the field, otherwise the analysis could be spurious, leading to dangerous components being manufactured.

If the intended component has a complicated cross-section, that is one that would make it difficult to calculate a possible structural performance as it is, a starting point for potential performance levels can be made with the available material data, modulus, strength, etc, using this to get a possible structural performance level for parts of the sectional shape.

For example, if the cross-section was in the form of a cross, as a starting point, it could be considered as a vertical member and a horizontal member. Use the cross-sectional dimensions of each to obtain a performance level, and add them together to give a 'ball park' guide to potential.

It must be remembered that the resultant performance level will not be exact, because two separate levels have been added together, but each could gain added advantage from the other. That is, the vertical member could have improved performance by receiving a stabilizing effect from the junction between the two members. This also applies, to some degree, to the horizontal member.

This simple method of arriving at an approximate performance level can be adopted for a wide range of cross-sections, but in some cases the stabilizing effect will be greater and result in a higher performance level. In others, the stabilizing or supporting effect will be less, resulting in a lower structural performance.

The foregoing will provide some starting points for a basic approach to composite design, but at this stage for simple laminated components only.

Many structural applications utilizing composites are based on sandwich structures–a core material in some form with skins of another material bonded, or formed, on to each side. This results in a very stiff, and often very light, panel or structure.

Sandwich structures can be simple flat panels and utilized in this form, using the previously-described cut-and-fold method of fabrication; or they could be moulded into many, and often complex, shapes. Core materials can be selected for this sandwich form to enhance the structural perform-

ABOVE FAR LEFT A typical test machine for gauging tensile, lap shear, peel strength, etc

ABOVE LEFT A close-up of the chucks shows a carbon fibre specimen under tension

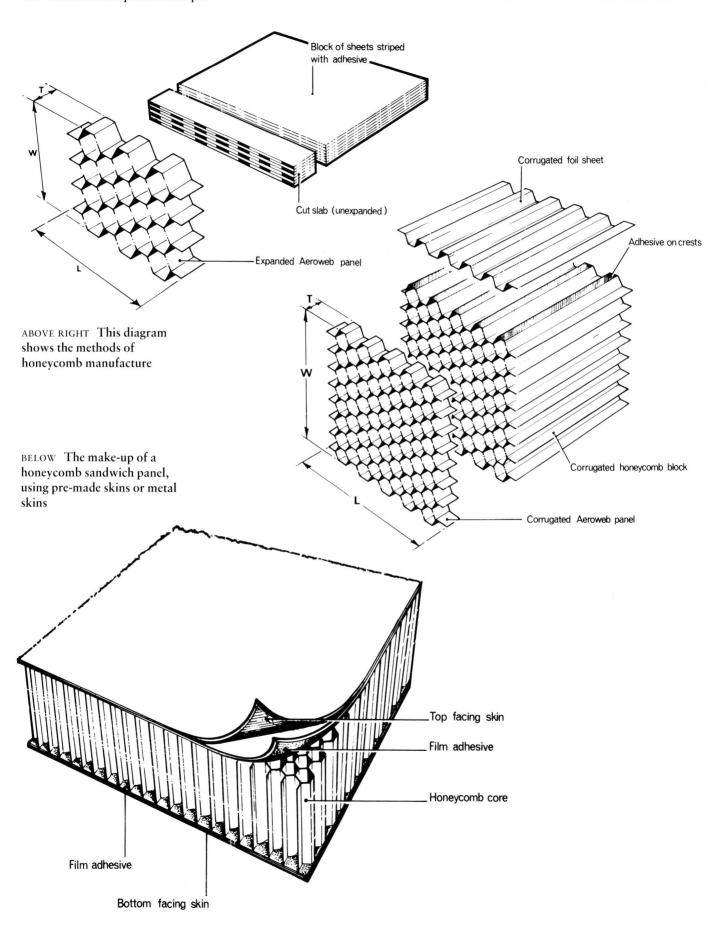

T
W
L

Block of sheets striped with adhesive

Cut slab (unexpanded)

Expanded Aeroweb panel

Corrugated foil sheet

Adhesive on crests

Corrugated honeycomb block

Corrugated Aeroweb panel

T
W
L

ABOVE RIGHT This diagram shows the methods of honeycomb manufacture

BELOW The make-up of a honeycomb sandwich panel, using pre-made skins or metal skins

Top facing skin

Film adhesive

Honeycomb core

Film adhesive

Bottom facing skin

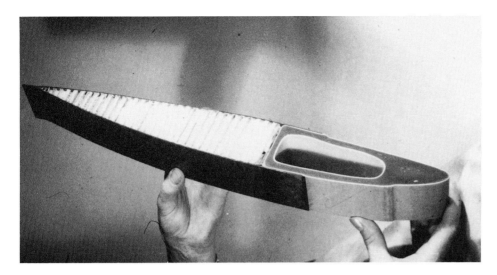

ance of a very wide range of components.

Sandwich construction can be used for a complex-shaped component by pre-machining the core material to shape. One very good example is the use of honeycomb as the core material for the many forms of aerofoil shape. In aircraft components, in many cases, the skin materials will be an alloy; in the downforce wings used on racing cars, the skins are usually carbon fibre.

The chassis of race cars, and now motorcycles, utilize machined honeycomb, as do many other commercial applications.

Designing for the use of core materials in complex-shaped components is very complicated. To arrive at a theoretical performance level, without the advantage of a full stress analysis, would involve calculating for sections of the overall shape. These would be used collectively, making allowance for the stabilizing effect of adjoining sections and for the presence of the core material.

Where sandwich structures are being used in place of a similar component manufactured from conventional materials, the task of design in composites is simplified by having a standard of performance to meet or improve on. However, where the composite component is an original concept, the design must begin with pure theory backed by proving test work.

A good example of machine-profiled honeycomb is shown in this section of helicopter rotor blade

Composite performance

As a measure of the effect that composite utilization can have on structural components, some comparisons with components previously manufactured from conventional materials will illustrate the potential.

A prime example is a single-seater racing-car chassis, or monocoque. For many years the tubular-steel space-frame was the universal method of construction. Towards the end of this chassis' period of manufacture, when all the experience was being utilized, the torsional stiffness of the structure was in the region of 2500 ft lb/degree. This would vary slightly from design to design.

The advent of the single-stressed-skin monocoque was to see torsional stiffness increased to approximately 3500 ft lb/degree and with a reduction in weight. The alloy-skinned monocoque was then to receive the first advantage from composites in the form of honeycomb. This was used between the skins. The stabilizing effect from this addition resulted in torsional stiffness rising to 5000 ft lb/degree.

The use of honeycomb in chassis, or monocoque, design was a significant step for composites, and was quickly followed up by designers who utilized composite skin materials to take monocoque performance a giant step forward, both in stiffness and strength.

Stiffness is always important for car performance, but the new strength levels were to produce much greater driver safety.

As a measure of the immense improvement in monocoque performance, a typical current Formula One car, which in most cases utilizes carbon fibre skins on honeycomb and manufactured by the moulding method, results in a torsional stiffness performance in the region of 10,000 ft lb/degree, coupled with immense strength.

In the case of motorcycle chassis or frames, the use of composites has had a similar effect on structural performance.

A prime example is the GP500 frame, an early tubular-steel type, which weighed in at approximately 10 kg. The use of alloy tube reduced the weight to the region of 7.5 kg, but, although 25 per cent lighter, the alloy version was somewhere in the region of 15 per cent less stiff. Changing to an alloy, fabricated, box-like spine or main member still produced a weight of 7.5 kg, but the new shape increased stiffness by up to 10 or 15 per cent when compared to the steel version.

A new chassis, manufactured from pre-made, flat, alloy-skinned honeycomb panels, weighed approximately 10.5 kg; quite heavy, but the stiffness showed an amazing 100 per cent improvement.

The follow-up version still used honeycomb sandwich panels, but the skins of the sandwich were made of carbon fibre. This resulted in a chassis weighing 8.9 kg and still 100 per cent better in stiffness than the best metallic chassis; the alloy spar tube at 8.76 kg.

Following this trend, designers will, with experience, optimize the use of composite materials.

Comparisons between the performances of aerospace components made in conventional materials and in composites are more difficult, due to the fact that components utilizing composites are designed specifically for those materials and may differ in layout, making direct comparisons impractical. This applies to both large aircraft and homebuilt types. In the case of the latter, and some small commercial aircraft, the aircraft itself will have been designed around the use of composite materials. Therefore, its configuration, from the structural aspect, may be totally different to what it would have been if made in conventional materials.

This serves to illustrate the point that composites can be designed to meet very many structural requirements, but these requirements must be known to the designer. Where there are no known structural requirement levels, calculation and test work must be used to arrive at both starting point and proposed structural component.

Where the component is a secondary structure, that is it may carry load, but is not a life-dependent structure, and where design would be difficult, the material, thickness, configuration, and any other aspects can be arrived at by a degree of trial and error. Many successful composite components have been made using this latter method.

Composite load-bearing structures can be designed to meet many needs and applications. They are becoming widely used as structure floors or platforms, especially where weight is a critical factor; examples are air-craft floors, transport where payload is important, and platforms, etc that are subject to movement.

The design of load-bearing, flat surfaces is more straightforward than complex shapes. The same design information is a great help when the design is to be a structure fabricated from a pre-made flat panel, or panels.

The following notes and diagrams, plus pages reproduced from Ciba-Geigy brochures (on pages 109–117), will assist the prospective designer in his effort to utilize composites in some areas. These, and the previously-mentioned design notes should provide a starting point for those wishing to begin to design in composite materials.

Multi-layer laminates in flexure

A common problem in the design of FRP composites is the analysis of laminates made up from layers of different materials. The two prime requirements are to determine the flexural rigidity and the strength of the composite.

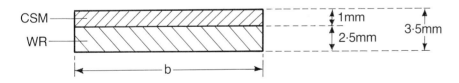

Fig. 1

A simple strength-of-materials approach is as follows:

A typical combination of materials is chopped-strand mat and woven roving.

Say a laminate consists simply of a thickness of each, as in Fig. 1 (note a 'thickness' may be made up from several layers of that material).

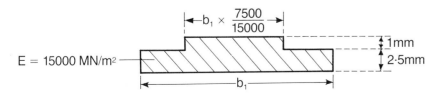

Fig. 2

Say E (CSM) = 7500 MN/m²
    E (WR) = 15,000 MN/m²

Fig. 3

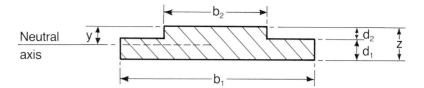

The flexural rigidity of the section may be found by the 'equivalent section' technique. In this method, a theoretical section shape is assumed and the thickness of each layer stays the same, but the width is determined by the elastic modulus of the layer. The second moment of area of the section may then be calculated. For instance, if the material is assumed to be all woven roving, then the equivalent section of Fig. 1 would be as shown in Fig. 2. The position of the neutral axis, the second moment of area and hence the flexural rigidity can be calculated thus (Fig. 3):

Fig. 4

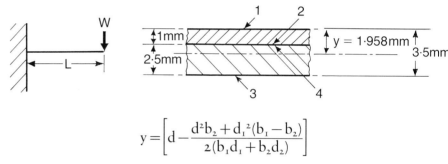

$$y = \left[d - \frac{d^2 b_2 + d_1^2 (b_1 - b_2)}{2(b_1 d_1 + b_2 d_2)} \right]$$

equation 1

Fig. 5

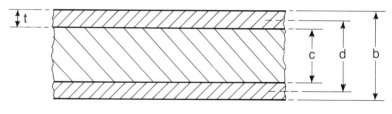

$$I = \tfrac{1}{3} [b_2 . y^3 + b_1 (d - y)^3 - (b_1 - b_2)(d - y - d_1)^3]$$

equation 2

hence

$$y = 3.5 - \frac{(3.5^2 \times .5 + 2.5^2 (.5))}{2(1 \times 2.5 + .5 \times 1)} = 1.958 \text{ mm}$$

$$I = \tfrac{1}{3} [.5 \times y^3 + 1 (3.5 - y)^3 - (.5)(3.5 - y - 2.5)^3] = 2.619 \text{ mm}^4$$

i.e. The second moment of area of the 'equivalent section' is 2.619 mm⁴
∴ EI (the flexural rigidity) of the actual section = 2.619 × 15,000 Nmm²
∴ EI = 39,285 Nmm²

The second part of the problem is strength. If the laminate is subjected to a bending moment, what will be the stress distribution and how will it fail?

Consider Fig. 4.

The stress at any distance C from the neutral axis is:

$$o = \frac{M_b \times C \times Ec}{EI}$$

where M = the applied bending moment

C = distance from the neutral axis

Ec = Elastic modulus of the material at position C

EI = overall flexural rigidity

Hence at position (1) $o_1 = \dfrac{M_b \times 1.958 \times 7500}{39,285} = 374 M_b$ N/mm²

at postition (2) $o_2 = \dfrac{M_b(1.958-1) \times 7500}{36,285} = 183 M_b$ N/mm²

at postition (3) $o_3 = \dfrac{M_b(1.958-1) \times 15,000}{39,285} = 366 M_b$ N/mm²

at postition (4) $o_4 = \dfrac{M_b(3.5-1.958) \times 15,000}{39,285} = 589 M_b$ N/mm²

It can be seen that the maximum stress is at position (4). This is not necessarily the most likely failure position, because at position (4) the material is woven roving which has higher strength than chopped-strand mat.

Say the chopped-strand mat ultimate strength, tensile or compressive, (ôCSM) = 104 MN/m²

and the woven roving ultimate strength, tensile or compressive, (ôWR) = 280 MN/m²

then equating stress and strength (o and ô), find the bending moment at which failure occurs (M_b) thus:

$$o_1 = \hat{o}CSM \therefore 374 M_b = 100 \therefore M_b = 267 \text{ Nmm}$$
$$o_2 = \hat{o}CSM \therefore 183 M_b = 100 \therefore M_b = 546 \text{ Nmm}$$
$$o_3 = \hat{o}WR \therefore 366 M_b = 280 \therefore M_b = 765 \text{ Nmm}$$
$$o_4 = \hat{o}WR \therefore 589 M_b = 280 \therefore M_b = 475 \text{ Nmm}$$

It can be seen that initial failure occurs at position (1), i.e. the outer face of the chopped-strand mat layer, when a bending moment of 267 Nmm is reached. Note, it has been assumed that tensile strength and compressive strength are equal. This is not necessarily so, in which case the direction of bend would alter the conditions, i.e. whether the critical positions were subjected to tensile or compressive loads.

Sandwich construction

Sandwich construction is an extremely effective method of producing stiff, light and cheap structures in FRP, when used in the right application and in the right manner. The following equations will assist with the less complex situations and should illustrate some of the problems which exist when designing sandwich structures.

Sandwich structures are generally used to improve the flexural-rigidity performance in terms of cost, or weight of a panel or beam. The use of

FRP in this manner is extremely efficient. Consider Fig. 5.

Various expressions may be used to determine the flexural rigidity of sandwich structures. Each has its own particular limitations. *Equation 3* ignores the flexural rigidity of the core, which is a reasonable assumption for many of the foam cores used with FRP, but would not be acceptable for a balsa core, which would itself have appreciable rigidity.

$$\text{flexural rigidity } D = \frac{E_s \times b(h^3 - c^3)}{12}$$

equation 3

where E_s = skin modulus
      b = width of the beam
If the flexural rigidity of the core is included, then the expression becomes:

$$D = E_s \frac{b.t^3}{6} + \frac{E_s.b.t.d^2}{2} + \frac{E_c.b.c^3}{12}$$

equation 4

The first two terms are another way of writing *equation 3*.

The third term relates to the flexural rigidity of the core.

E_s and E_c are the elastic modulii of skins and core respectively. The first term in the above expression may be ignored if the skins are thin. The third may be ignored if the bending stiffness of the core is small. Consequently, a reasonable approximation under the right conditions is:

$$D = \frac{E_s \times b.t.d^2}{2}$$

equation 5

Therefore, use *equation 4* if the core has appreciable stiffness and the skins are thick. Use *equation 3* if the skins are again thick, but the core has negligible rigidity. Use *equation 5* if the skins are thin and the core has negligible rigidity.

Very often, the designer is able to ignore shear deflections but, unfortunately, sandwich structures are particularly prone to this problem and shear deflections must be determined.

For a simply supported sandwich beam with a load W in the centre, the deflection due to shear is given by:

$$\text{o shear} = \frac{W\,L.c}{4.b\,d^2.G}$$

and for simple support with a uniformly distributed load of w/unit length

$$\text{o shear} = \frac{w\,L^2.c}{8.b\,d^2.G}$$

where L = span
      G = shear modulus of the core.

Example

Determine the total deflection of the sandwich beam shown in Fig. 6.
Using the more rigorous expression for flexural rigidity 'D'.

$$D = \frac{E_s.b.t^3}{6} + \frac{E_s.b.t.d^2}{2} + \frac{E_c.b.c^3}{12} =$$

$$\frac{7000 \times 100 \times 3^3}{6} + \frac{7000 \times 100 \times 3 \times 28^2}{2} + \frac{20 \times 100 \times 25^3}{12}$$

$$= 3.15 \times 10^6 + 823 \times 10^6 + 2.604 \times 10^6$$

$$\therefore D = 828 \times 10^6 \text{ N.mm}^2$$

Note, in this case, the middle term of the expression alone gives an answer with less than one per cent error.

Now total deflection = deflection due to bending plus bending due to shear.

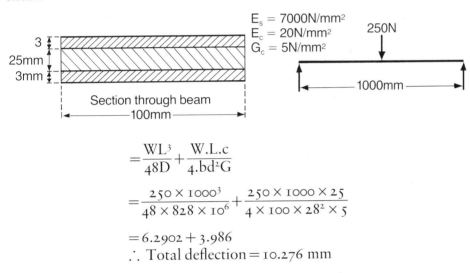

$E_s = 7000\text{N/mm}^2$
$E_c = 20\text{N/mm}^2$
$G_c = 5\text{N/mm}^2$

250N

1000mm

3
25mm
3mm

Section through beam
100mm

Fig. 6

$$= \frac{WL^3}{48D} + \frac{W.L.c}{4.bd^2G}$$

$$= \frac{250 \times 1000^3}{48 \times 828 \times 10^6} + \frac{250 \times 1000 \times 25}{4 \times 100 \times 28^2 \times 5}$$

$$= 6.2902 + 3.986$$

$$\therefore \text{ Total deflection} = 10.276 \text{ mm}$$

Stresses in sandwich beams

The actual bending stresses in sandwich beams are illustrated in Fig. 7, but it is reasonable to assume that the core carries none of the bending stress and that the skins have a constant stress through their thickness. Hence the bending stresses may be assumed to be as is shown in Fig. 8.

The actual shear stresses in a sandwich beam are as shown in Fig. 9, but it is reasonable to assume that the stresses are as shown in Fig. 10.

The actual bending stress in the skins is given by:

$$o_s = \frac{M.E_s.h}{2D}$$

equation 6

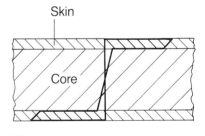

Skin

Core

Fig. 7

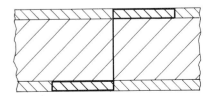

Fig. 8

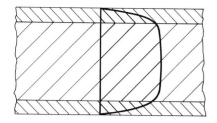

Fig. 9

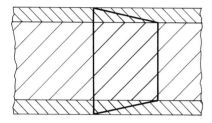

Fig. 10

but if D is taken from *equation 5*, then

$$o_s = \frac{M.h}{b.t.d^2}$$

equation 7

where M is the applied bending moment.

The actual shear stress in the core (T_c) is given by:

$$T_c = \frac{Q}{D}\left\{E_s.t.\frac{d}{2} + \frac{E_c}{2}\left(\frac{c^2}{4} - y^2\right)\right\}$$

equation 8

where y is any distance from the neutral axis and Q is the shear force. If, however, E_c is assumed to be zero and *equation 5* is again taken for D, then the shear stress in the core is:

$$T_c = \frac{Q}{b.d}$$

equation 9

Example

Determine the bending stress in the skin and the shear stress in the core for the beam illustrated in the previous example.

The bending stress in the skins is:

$$o_s = \frac{M.h}{b.t.d^2}$$

$$M = \frac{250}{2}\frac{1000}{2}\ N.mm$$

$$h = 31\ mm$$
$$b = 100\ mm$$
$$t = 3\ mm$$
$$d = 28\ mm$$

$$\therefore o_s = \frac{250 \times 1000}{2 \times 2} \times \frac{31}{100 \times 3 \times 28^2} = 8.24\ N/mm^2$$

the shear stress in the core $T_c = \frac{Q}{b.d}$

$$\therefore T_c = \frac{250}{2 \times 100 \times 28} = .045\ N/mm^2$$

Structural Honeycomb Sandwich Design

The honeycomb sandwich beam is analogous to the "I"-beam, (diag. 1) with its facing skins replacing the flanges to carry bending stresses and the honeycomb core replacing the web across the whole width of the beam to resist shearing stresses, and at the same time stabilising the skins to inhibit buckling (the "I"-beam's buckling resistance has to be carried in the flanges).

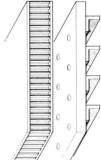

Diag. 1

Diag. 2

Similarly, the honeycomb sandwich panel can be compared with a stiffened panel as shown in diag. 2. In addition to the advantages of honeycomb sandwich mentioned earlier in this brochure, it can also be seen that stiffening (stabilisation) is achieved across the whole of the panel and in all directions (although not equally since honeycomb is stronger in one direction than the other—approx. 2:1).

General

The number of variables within a honeycomb sandwich panel (core thickness, core density, skin thickness, skin material) and the many external design influences preclude the existence of a fully comprehensive design manual to define fully any honeycomb sandwich panel a designer may need— the shape, profile, loading conditions, space restrictions etc. in short, the variety of design parameters is enormous.

In the following pages of this brochure, then, only general, flat, honeycomb sandwich design is considered, and in a very simplified way so that engineers who are not familiar with this type of construction can make a first approximation to panel design.

A follow-up publication is available, on request, which gives a simplified method for the designer to check this first approximation of design theoretically However, a large degree of design empiricism must remain. Any theoretical solution tends to give adequate but flimsy structures, with thick core and very thin skins—impractical if fittings have to be attached to the panel. In fact, second order requirements very often dictate the design of the sandwich e.g. the need to have melamine decorative surfaces for easy cleaning; the melamine could be used as the skin material but might over-design the panel from a strength point of view.

To find—skin thickness, core thickness, core density

Three basic design conditions are considered here :-

(a) Beams, under various loading and support conditions

(b) Panels, under uniform normal pressure and simply supported edges

(c) Panels, under end compressive loads with simply supported edges and fixed edges

Step 1 In each case, the first step is to calculate the beam or panel stiffness (EI).

In condition (a), $EI = \dfrac{K.P.L^3}{\delta}$

where K is obtained from table 1, and δ is the designer's acceptable level of deflection

In condition (b), consider a unit element across the shorter dimension of the panel and treat as a beam in (a) above

In condition (c), with simply supported loading edges

$$EI = \frac{P.L^2}{\pi^2}$$

and with fixed loading edges

$$EI = \frac{4P.L^2}{9\pi^2}$$

Step 2 Having calculated the stiffness, the second step is to use that value in figure 1 to select skin thickness and honeycomb core thickness.

(Enter the graph along the reference axis until the calculated EI value is reached. Move diagonally to the line corresponding to the modulus of elasticity of the skin material — glass fibre, 3; aluminium 10; steel, 30, etc. (on the imperial units figure). Move vertically until the skin thickness lines are reached. Choose a skin thickness and read off the corresponding core thickness on the left hand axis).

Note : Generally, more evenly distributed loads require a thinner skin, and more concentrated loads require a thicker skin.

Step 3 For cases (a) and (b), calculate the maximum design shear stress, using table 1 and the relationship.

shear stress = $\dfrac{\text{shear load (V)}}{\text{x-sect. area}}$ (where the x-sectional area is the gross core x-section and not the net area of the foil in either direction). Then from table 2, choose the core type which will withstand that stress.

In case (c), the core is assumed not to take any of the applied compressive load and should be chosen to meet secondary conditions (in the case of load-supporting bulkheads, for instance, due consideration should be given to accidental bumps against the face of the panel). Also, shear stress induced by imperfect top and bottom edge fittings should be considered.

Figure 1 (Imperial Units)

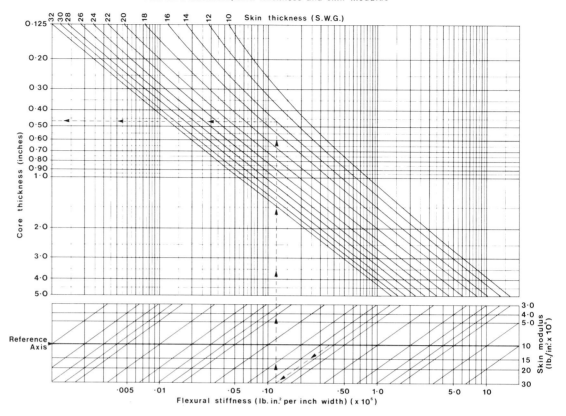

Variations of sandwich flexural stiffness (E I)
with core thickness, skin thickness and skin modulus

Figure 1 (Metric Units)

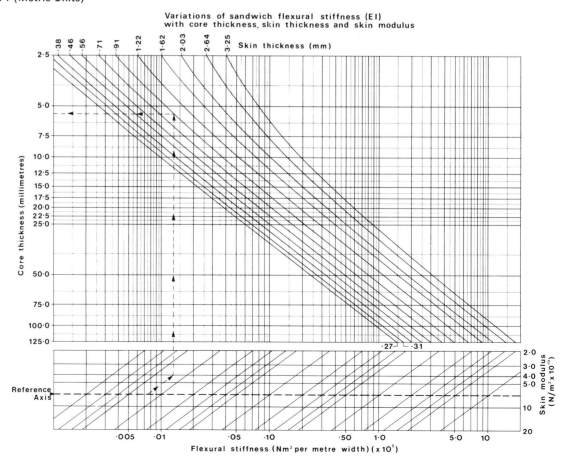

Variations of sandwich flexural stiffness (E I)
with core thickness, skin thickness and skin modulus

Honeycomb Sandwich Design

The proceeding 5 pages gave an introduction to Aeroweb honeycomb sandwich structures—their construction, applications, and a simple technique for making a first approximation to their design.—core thickness, skin thickness, and core density.

This follow-on presents a straightforward technique for checking that initial design under the most common loading conditions, to ensure that deflection, stresses in facing skins, and core shear stresses do not exceed acceptable levels.

Summary of possible failure modes

Honeycomb sandwich structures can fail in a number of characteristic modes which depend upon the relative sizes and material properties of the component parts of the sandwich and are shown below.

(a) Local crushing of core

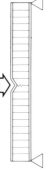

This takes place when an excessive local load is concentrated on the sandwich. Failure is caused by low core compression strength. Cure is to use core of higher density, either locally or throughout the panel, depending upon circumstances.

(b) Indentation of skin

Associated with impact loads with sharp corners. Increase skin thickness or use gfrp skins which are more resilient than aluminium skins.

(c) Transverse shear failure

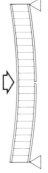

This occurs in honeycomb sandwich beams or panels which have insufficient core shear strength or panel thickness. Check original design in sheet 2 (for beams) or sheet 3 (for panels) in conjunction with the Aeroweb design factor in sheet 1.

(d) Facing skin failure

This normally occurs as a tensile failure in a very thin facing skin on ultra lightweight beams and is cured by increasing the skin or core thickness. Check original design in sheet 2 in conjunction with the Aeroweb design factor in sheet 1.

(e) General buckling

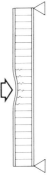

This is an overall Euler-type instability and is caused by insufficient panel thickness or core shear rigidity.

Table 1

Type of Beam	Maximum Shear V	Bending Constant K
	$\frac{P}{2}$	$\frac{1}{48}$
	$\frac{P}{2}$	$\frac{1}{192}$
	$\frac{P}{2}$	$\frac{11}{768}$
P = pL	$\frac{P}{2}$	$\frac{5}{384}$
P = pL	$\frac{P}{2}$	$\frac{1}{389}$
P	P	$\frac{1}{3}$
P = pL	P	$\frac{1}{8}$

Table 2

Some Typical Honeycomb Types

	Product Designation	Shear Stress (kN/m²)	Density (kg/m³)
Aeroweb Type 3003	2.3–3/8–15	550	37
	3.4–1/4–15	960	54
	3.7–1/8–25	1170	59
	5.2–1/8–25	1950	83
	7.1–1/8–15	3310	114
Aeroweb Type 5052	2.3–1/4–10	690	37
	3.1–1/6–10	1070	50
	3.4–1/4–15	1240	54
	4.3–1/8–20	1830	69
	4.5–1/8–10	1970	72
	5.2–1/4–25	2480	83
	7.9–1/8–40	4480	126
Aeroweb Type A1	A1–24–6	340	24
	A1–32–6	550	32
	A1–48–5	1240	48
	A1–64–5	1720	64
	A1–29–5(OX)	340	29
	A1–48–6(OX)	690	48

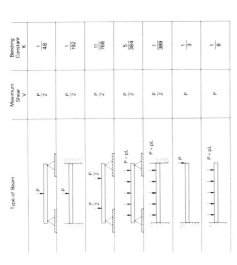

Shear stress figures are representative of strengths in ribbon direction which should be used parallel to longest side of beam or shortest side of panel.

Other densities are available—

Overexpanded core (OX) is particularly suitable for single curvature constructions.

How to use the design checking sheets

The following parts have been specially prepared in order to continue the easy and straightforward approach to the design of Aeroweb honeycomb sandwich started in part I of this brochure. To use them the Aeroweb Design Factor A_w must first be found from sheet I. Then all that is required is simply to substitute the design parameters into formulae given, using constants read from the accompanying graphs where appropriate.

Sheet 1 Aeroweb Design Factor A_w—for aluminium or *Nomex honeycombs
Sheet 2 Simply supported sandwich beams—deflection, core shear stress, facing skin stress
Sheet 3 Simply supported rectangular sandwich panels—deflection, core shear stress, facing skin stress
Sheet 4 Buckling stress in compression—simply supported edges, fixed edges

*Nomex is a Du Pont Trademark

PART 1—AEROWEB Design Factor, A_w

Aeroweb Design Factor A_w is a measure of the rigidity of a sandwich panel in flexure in relation to its rigidity in shear. This factor is used to simplify the stressing calculations for Aeroweb cored sandwich panels described in the following sheets.

Information required for the determination of factor A_w for each specific problem is as follows:

t = thickness of facing skins

c = thickness of core

y = characteristic length of sandwich panel. The appropriate dimension to be taken as the characteristic length, y, is given on each of the following sheets

The nomograms have been constructed on the assumption that the facing skins are of equal thickness. For sandwich panels with facing skins of unequal thickness take

$$t = \frac{2t_1 . t_2}{t_1 + t_2}$$

where t_1, and t_2, are the thicknesses of the upper and lower facing skins respectively.

The assumption has also been made that the facing skins are of aluminium alloy with a modulus of elasticity of 10×10^6 lb/in² For panels with facing skins of another material the value of A_w obtained from the nomogram must be multiplied by the factor

$$\frac{\text{modulus of elasticity of facing skin material}}{\text{modulus of elasticity of aluminium}}$$

How to use the Aeroweb Design Factor Nomograms (opposite)

On the left side of the relevant nomogram plot a point Q whose co-ordinates are (i) the calculated value of $\frac{c}{t}$ and (ii) the density of the core to be used.

On the right side of the same nomogram plot a point P whose co-ordinates are (i) the calculated value of $\frac{y}{c}$ and (ii) the same density of core to be used.

The line joining these two points crosses the A_w scale at R, indicating the Aeroweb Design Factor value for use in the following sheets.

(f) Shear buckling

Occurs as a result of low core shear modulus or shear strength, and usually follows as a consequence of general Euler type buckling. Check original design in sheet 4 in conjunction with the Aeroweb design factor in sheet 1.

(g) Face wrinkling

This is a rather involved mode of failure and depends upon the core elastic and compression properties and the initial waviness of the facing material. The mode of failure is characterised by the local buckling of one or both facings into or away from the core. The direction of failure (into or away from the core) depends upon the relative tensile strength of the skin-to-core adhesive and the compression strength of the core.

The wrinkling phenomenon is more usually associated with sandwich structures containing plastic foam or balsa wood core and seldom occurs with a honeycomb core, except in the case of short column buckling.

For practical design purposes the following simple expression is used to give wrinkling stress values for a perfectly flat sandwich panel:

$$\sigma_{wi} = 0.50 \ (G_c E_c E_f)^{\frac{1}{3}} \quad \text{———(1)}$$

Normal production irregularities such as slight surface waviness and core property variation cause a decrease of critical wrinkling stress of approx 20–30 per cent.

If the wrinkling stress exceeds the proportional limit of the facing skin material, then the facing modulus E_f in equation (1) must be replaced by a reduced modulus E_r. It is suggested that a suitable form is:

$$E_r = \frac{4E_f E_t}{(E_f + E_t)^2} \quad \text{———(2)}$$

The application of equation (1) then requires a series of successive approximations to give the wrinkling stress. A more straightforward, although conservative, approach is simply to take $E_f = E_t$ (tangent modulus).

(h) Intercell buckling (face dimpling)

The faces of a honeycomb sandwich panel when loaded in bending or column compression may show a pattern of dimples the size of the honeycomb cells. This dimpling is essentially the buckling of the facing material over the area of each honeycomb cell, acting as a simply supported hexagonal plate under compression.

A reasonable estimation of inter-cell buckling stress is given by the following:

$$\sigma_{cr} = 3E_f \left(\frac{t}{d}\right)^2 \quad \text{———(3)}$$

where d is the diameter of a circle inscribed within the hexagonal cell and the reduced modulus E_f is considered to equal the tangent modulus E_t. Inter-cell buckling is usually restricted to panels with extremely thin facing skins and large cell sizes, and for most practical applications this mode of failure is unlikely. Indeed, in some sandwich panel designs it is very difficult to manufacture the panels without "telegraphing" i.e. the honeycomb cell shape showing through the skin, yet although this should theoretically reduce the critical buckling stress considerably, the panels very seldom fail because of that.

Sheet 2 — SIMPLY SUPPORTED SANDWICH BEAMS with AEROWEB cores

Enlarged view of element of beam

diagram 1

L = semi-span of beam.

a = distance of concentrated load from centre line of beam (see diagram 2b).

b = $L - a$ = distance of concentrated load from adjacent support.

e = width of beam.

t_1 = thickness of upper facing skin.

t_2 = thickness of lower facing skin.

c = thickness of core.

d = $c + \dfrac{t_1 + t_2}{2}$ = distance between median planes of facing skins.

y = characteristic length (used in determining A_w) to be taken as $y = L$ = semi-span of beam for the calculations described on this sheet.

A_w = Aeroweb Design Factor (from sheet 1).

w = load per unit span for beam with uniformly distributed load.

P = magnitude of each load for beam with concentrated loads.

E = modulus of elasticity of facing skin material.

δ = normal deflection of beam at its centre.

a) Beam with uniformly distributed load

diagram 2

b) Beam with two concentrated loads

NORMAL DEFLECTION

For a simply supported beam with a uniformly distributed load the deflection at the centre of the beam is given by:

$$\delta = \frac{L^4(t_1 + t_2)}{ed^2t_1t_2}\frac{w}{E}\,C_1$$

where C_1 is obtained from diagram 3.

For a simply supported beam with two symmetrically disposed concentrated loads each of magnitude P, the deflection at the centre of the beam is given by:

$$\delta = \frac{b^3(t_1 + t_2)}{ed^2t_1t_2}\frac{P}{E}\,C_2$$

where C_2 is obtained from diagram 4.

For a simply supported beam with a single central concentrated load, a is zero and P is taken as half the central load.

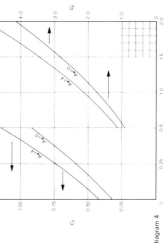

diagram 3

diagram 4

The curves presented here have been derived for the usual arrangement in which the longitudinal core direction is along the length of the beam. For cases where the longitudinal core direction is across the width of the beam the value of A_w should be multiplied by 1·5.

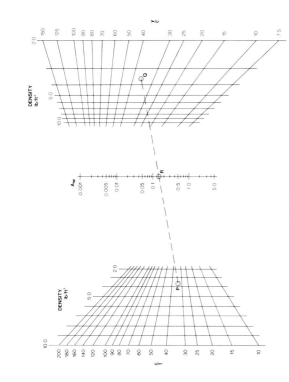

Aeroweb ALUMINIUM Honeycomb Design Factor

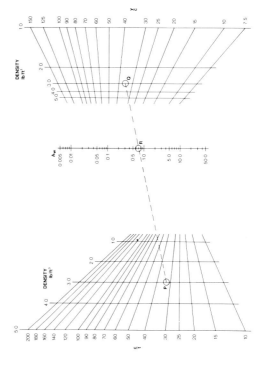

Aeroweb NOMEX Honeycomb Design Factor

Sheet 3 — SIMPLY SUPPORTED RECTANGULAR SANDWICH PANELS with AEROWEB cores under uniform normal pressure

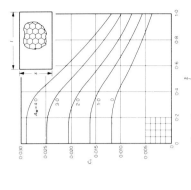

diagram 1

l = length of longer side of panel

s = length of shorter side of panel

t_1 = thickness of upper facing skin

t_2 = thickness of lower facing skin

c = thickness of core

$d = c + \dfrac{t_1 + t_2}{2}$ = distance between median planes of facing skins

A_w = Aeroweb Design Factor (from sheet 1)

y = characteristic length (used in determining A_w) to be taken as
$\qquad y = s$ = length of shorter side of panel
$\qquad$ for the calculations described on this sheet

E = modulus of elasticity of facing skin material

p = normal pressure

δ = normal deflection of panel at its centre

NORMAL DEFLECTION

For a simply supported rectangular panel under uniform normal pressure the deflection at the centre is given by:

$$\delta = \frac{s^4}{EJ}\, p\, C_1 \qquad \text{where} \qquad J = \frac{t_1\, t_2}{t_1 + t_2}\, d^2 \qquad \text{and } C_1 \text{ is obtained from the appropriate}$$

graph below, depending on the core ribbon direction.

diagram 2

diagram 3

Note: For interpolation the variation between A_w values shown may be taken as linear.

STRESSES IN FACING SKINS

f_1 = spanwise stress in upper facing skin

f_2 = spanwise stress in lower facing skin

For a simply supported beam with a uniformly distributed load the maximum values of f_1 and f_2 are given by:

$$f_1 = \frac{wL^2}{2edt_1}\left[1 + \frac{t_1}{2d}\left(1 + \frac{t_1}{t_2}\right)\right] \quad \text{and} \quad f_2 = \frac{wL^2}{2edt_2}\left[1 + \frac{t_2}{2d}\left(1 + \frac{t_2}{t_1}\right)\right]$$

These values of stress occur at the centre of the beam.

For a simply supported beam with two symmetrically disposed concentrated loads each of magnitude P the spanwise stresses in the facing skins are constant between the loads, and the maximum values are given by:

$$f_1 = \frac{Pb}{edt_1}\left[1 + \frac{t_1}{2d}\left(1 + \frac{t_1}{t_2}\right)\right] \quad \text{and} \quad f_2 = \frac{Pb}{edt_2}\left[1 + \frac{t_2}{2d}\left(1 + \frac{t_2}{t_1}\right)\right]$$

For a beam with a single central concentrated load, a is zero and P is taken as half the central load.

In each of the above cases the spanwise stress in the upper facing skin is compressive and in the lower skin it is tensile.

In general, the stresses vary through the thickness of the facing skins, the maximum values occuring at the top surface of the upper skin and at the bottom surface of the lower skin. In some cases the assumption of constant stress through the thickness of the skins will not introduce any appreciable error, and the term in square brackets may then be taken as unity. Such an assumption is permissible for beams with relatively thin facing skins, or when the elastic limit of the facing skin is well exceeded.

In close proximity to a concentrated load or support, the stress distribution is modified and stresses may occur that are somewhat different from the values given by using the formulae in this sheet.

CORE SHEAR STRESS

q = spanwise core shear stress

Q = maximum shear force on the beam

The maximum value of the spanwise core shear stress is given by:

$$q = \frac{Q}{ed}$$

The shear stress value is based on the gross area of the core and not on the net area of the foil.

For a simply supported beam with a uniformly distributed load
$$Q = wL$$

whereas for a simply supported beam with two symmetrically disposed concentrated loads each of magnitude P,
$$Q = P$$

For a beam with a single central concentrated load, a is zero and P is taken as half the central load.

In close proximity to a concentrated load or support, the stress distribution is modified and stresses may occur that are somewhat different from the values given by this sheet.

STRESSES IN FACING SKINS

f_l = stress in facing skin in direction parallel to longer side of panel

f_s = stress in facing skin in direction parallel to shorter side of panel

For the upper facing skin of a simply supported rectangular sandwich panel under uniform normal pressure the maximum value of stress in the direction parallel to the long side of the panel is given by:

$$f_l = \frac{s^2}{d\,t_1}\,p\,C_2$$

and that in the direction parallel to the short side of the panel is given by:

$$f_s = \frac{s^2}{d\,t_1}\,p\,C_3$$

where C_2 and C_3 are obtained from the appropriate graph below, depending on the core ribbon direction.

For the lower facing skin the stresses are obtained by substituting t_2 for t_1 in the expressions given above.

The stresses in the upper facing skin (i.e. that on which the uniform normal pressure is acting) are compressive; in the lower facing skin they are tensile. In both cases the maximum stress in the skin occurs at the centre of the panel.

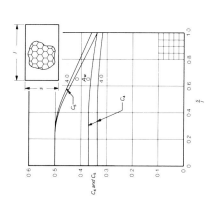

diagram 4

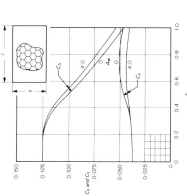

diagram 5

Note: For interpolation the variation between A_w values shown may be taken as linear.

CORE SHEAR STRESSES

q_l = core shear stress in a plane parallel to the longer side of the panel

q_s = core shear stress in a plane parallel to the shorter side of the panel

For a simply supported rectangular panel under uniform normal pressure the maximum value of core shear stress in a plane parallel to the long side of the panel is given by:

$$q_l = \frac{s}{d}\,p\,C_4$$

and that in a plane parallel to the short side of the panel is given by:

$$q_s = \frac{s}{d}\,p\,C_5$$

where C_4 and C_5 are obtained from the appropriate graph below, depending on the core ribbon direction.

The maximum value of q_l occurs at the centre of the shorter edges of the panel and maximum value of q_s occurs at the centre of the longer edges.

It should be noted that the shear stress is based on the gross cross-section of the core and not on the net area of the foil in either direction.

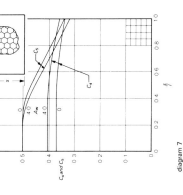

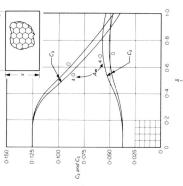

diagram 6

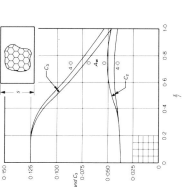

diagram 7

Note: For interpolation the variation between A_w values shown may be taken as linear.

Sheet 4 — BUCKLING STRESS IN COMPRESSION for flat rectangular sandwich panels with AEROWEB cores

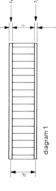

diagram 1

a = length of panel in direction of applied compression

b = width of panel

t_1 = thickness of upper facing skin

t_2 = thickness of lower facing skin

c = thickness of Aeroweb core

$d = c + \dfrac{t_1 + t_2}{2}$ = distance between median planes of facing skins

A_w = Aeroweb Design Factor (from sheet 1)

y = characteristic length (used in determining A_w), to be taken as

$$y = b = \text{width of panel}$$

for the calculations described on this sheet

E = modulus of elasticity of facing skin material

K = buckling stress coefficient

f_b = compressive stress in the facing skins when panel first buckles

Many panels loaded principally in compression will have facing skins of equal thickness, that is

$$t_1 = t_2$$

and in this case the expression for f_b simplifies to :

$$f_b = \left(\frac{d}{b}\right)^2 EK$$

for both the design cases on this sheet.

In plotting the accompanying graphs the kinks which would normally be present in curves of buckling stress against panel aspect ratio have been smoothed out by taking lower envelopes to the curves.

It should be noted that the honeycomb core is assumed not to take any of the applied compressive load and, therefore, at the onset of buckling, the compressive load acting along the edge of the panel is $f_b(t_1 + t_2)$ per unit width of the panel.

For buckling at stresses greater than the proportional limit it is suggested that an estimate of the buckling stress can be obtained by replacing E in the appropriate expression for f_b by E_t, the tangent modulus of elasticity of the facing skin material corresponding to the stress f_b.

SIMPLY SUPPORTED EDGES

For a simply supported flat rectangular sandwich panel the buckling stress in compression is given by :

$$f_b = \frac{4t_1 t_2}{(t_1 + t_2)^2}\left(\frac{d}{b}\right)^2 EK$$

where K is obtained from the appropriate graph below, depending on the core ribbon direction.

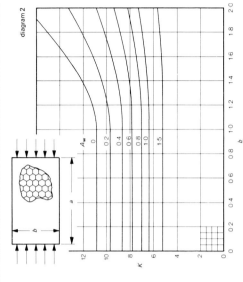

diagram 2

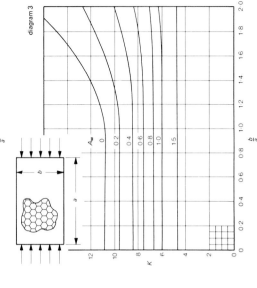

diagram 3

FIXED EDGES

For a flat rectangular sandwich panel with fixed edges, the buckling stress in compression is given by :

$$f_b = \frac{4t_1 t_2}{(t_1 + t_2)^3}\left(\frac{d}{b}\right)^2 EK$$

where K is obtained from the appropriate graph below, depending on the core ribbon direction.

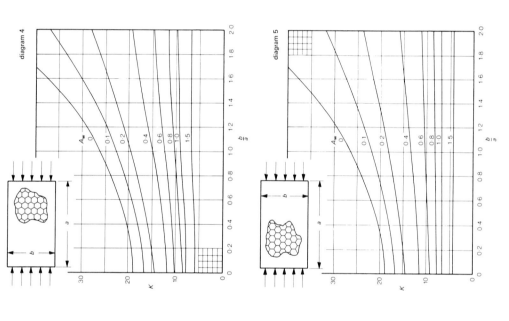

diagram 4

diagram 5

7 Composite repairs

The versatility of composites from the manufacturing point of view is well proven, as this book illustrates, but this versatility extends to the repair of composite components. The adhesive nature of many resin systems, coupled with the suitability of many cured composites to being bonded, often render these materials ideal for repair.

The repair method and material used will depend on various parameters, such as whether the component is structural or not. If it is, the repair must be aimed at retaining the structural integrity of the component. If the application is non-structural, it may be a question of finish. Can the aesthetic aspect be maintained, and will the repair have sufficient environmental resistance to maintain its performance or appearance?

Consideration must be given to whether or not the component was originally cured at elevated temperature. If it was, has it been incorporated into a much larger component, or have other parts been added that have little or no temperature resistance so that the intended repair can only be carried out using room-temperature curing systems? In this case, will the repair meet the required environmental performance and, very important, can the repair be carried out if the component is in situ? What type of repair is possible in this latter situation?

Most of these aspects of repair work can be overcome utilizing the versatility of composite materials.

Full details of all the possible permutations of composite repair would fill a large volume on their own. However, the methods of repairing composites are, to a great degree, a matter of using common sense, aided by the fact that if the constructor has sufficient skill and knowledge to manufacture the composite component, the method of repair would be a natural follow-on. Consequently, it is only intended to give some repair guidelines in this book.

With simple, impact-type damage, resulting in dents or minor tears and fractures on non-structural components, such as body panels, repair would merely be a matter of filling the dent or damaged area with a suitable filler. Where possible, it is advisable to make the repair with a similar resin type to that used in the original component, that is polyester, epoxy, etc.

If the component is of thin section, in many cases, the impact will damage the resin component of the laminate, and filling the recess would be a simple and efficient method of making good the damage. If, however, the fibre content has been damaged, it is advisable to laminate a patch over the back of the damaged area to restore the stiffness. Epoxy resin should be used for this patch, even on polyester components, since its adhesive qualities will render the repair more reliable.

The patch-type of repair can be used successfully to repair holes passing right through the laminate, or tears and splits. In the case, of large holes or splits, it is important that the laminated patch is as thick as the original component. In all cases, carry out some form of abrasion on the surface prior to laminating.

There may be situations where laminated composite components needing repair were originally cured at elevated temperature to meet a specification, aerospace components, for example. In this case, any repair must be of similar standard, which means it will have to be made with similar materials at the same, or similar, temperature cure cycle.

If the component is small, or can be removed from its location, sometimes the repair can be carried out in the original mould. In most cases, however, this is not possible, so the repair must be carried out in situ.

First, the extent of the damaged area must be established. This forms the basis of the size of the proposed repair area. There is no fixed rule for the size of the repair in relation to the damage but, as a guide, for dents or holes, the patch should be in the region of $2\frac{1}{2}$ times larger than the damaged area. For splits or cracks, the repair should extend no less than 30–35 mm ($1\frac{1}{4}$–$1\frac{1}{2}$ in.) on each side of the crack or split.

Whatever the repair material, that is wet resin and fabric or pre-preg, when repairing splits or cracks it is advisable to run a fine saw or cutter along the split. This will allow resin from the repair to penetrate fully.

Where possible, especially on multi-layer laminates, it is advisable to patch both sides, the repair becoming a crack stopper. However, this can be a problem if the outer face is surface critical, that is its surface finish must be maintained. If this is the case, where the laminate thickness allows, part of the laminate can be removed around the repair area. This should be up to 50 per cent of the original laminate thickness. The original thickness, or more, is then made up by a laminated patch on the other side.

If the component is to be repaired in the original mould, then the surface finish will be reproduced automatically. Where the repair is open, or free, the outer layers of the repair must be increased to allow for mechanical surface finishing.

These basic repair principles apply for both wet lay-up and pre-preg, whether cured at room temperature or elevated temperature.

Better results will be achieved when pressure is applied during the cure of the repair. This pressure, of course, is essential when pre-pregs are being used or a high-performance repair is required. In some cases, mechanical pressure may be possible, but where complex shapes are involved, the use of vacuum bags, as described previously, is ideal. On large components, the vacuum bag can often be sealed to the component itself, rather like a large patch around the repair area; smaller components can be placed inside a tailor-made bag.

In many cases, the materials forming the repair require elevated-temperature curing, in which case they must be selected so that the cure temperature will not degrade the original component. This can then be put back into a suitable oven for curing.

Where the component is too large, or is attached to something else, preventing it from being put into an oven, the required temperature can be achieved by the use of a heater box. This is made to cover the repair area, simply held in place over the repair, and then heated by electrical means or blown hot air. However, a widely used method of providing localized heating is by the use of commercial heater mats. These operate on the same principle as domestic electric blankets, but are capable of producing a much higher temperature. The mat is placed over the air-bleed layer, but under the vacuum bag, and with vacuum applied, the heater mat effects the cure.

These basic principles can be utilized to carry out a very wide range of repairs. A key point to remember is cleanliness, which includes general pre-treatment, that is surface abrasion, followed by a solvent wipe. Where material is being machined away to make room for the repair, the surface will be prepared automatically.

If a laminated patch (wet lay-up or pre-preg) is being placed on a surface, each patch layer should be cut slightly smaller than the previous one. This results in a laminate patch with a tapering edge thickness, which prevents a prominent step but, more importantly serves to minimize stress build-up at the edge of the repair.

Times and temperatures necessary to effect the correct cure will be found in the supplier's data sheet.

Where repairs are necessary on sandwich structures, there are additional points to consider.

First, and very important, is how deep into the sandwich the damage extends, and whether it affects one or both skins. How important is the core from the structural point of view? What is the core material, and what are the skin materials?

If the damage is of the impact type, resulting in some form of indentation, it is important to establish the extent of the damage to the core. In the case of aluminium honeycomb, deformation may have taken place. If this is slight, such as a depth of two or three times the skin thickness, in most cases, simply filling the dent will produce a satisfactory repair, especially if the skins are also aluminium. Where the core is Nomex, the resilience of this type of core resists impact damage better than aluminium.

Where a foam core is used, the important consideration is the extent to which the structural integrity depends on the core. For example, where

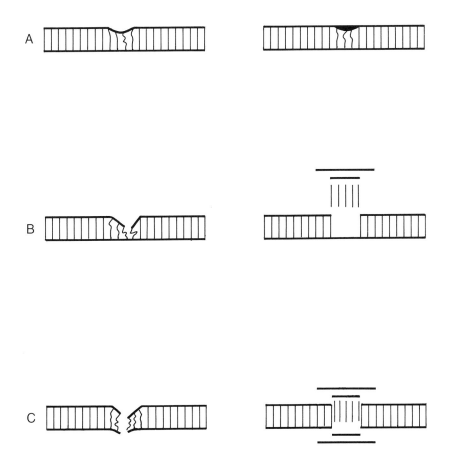

Repair methods for sandwich structures:
A Indentation type damage can be repaired using a suitable filler
B With damage that results in a breakthrough of one skin and crushing of the core, a borer is used to remove the damaged skin and core. A new piece of core is fitted into the hole, then a piece of skin material is cut to fit the hole. A larger piece covers that to spread the load
C Where the damage affects both skins, use the procedure outlined above, applying patches to each side
Repairs to composite structures are easy to carry out successfully, but do need attention to points such as pre-treatment to the repair area and the most suitable adhesive to meet the required performance level. If these points are observed, repairs can be carried out on almost any type of composite metallic or non-metallic, flat or contoured component. If the repair is carried out using elevated-temperature-cure adhesive, the component can be put in an oven, or where this is not possible, heater mats can be used. Also, vacuum can be utilized as a means of applying pressure, using the same method as for the manufacture of components. Similar methods can be used for laminated component repairs.

the core is used for insulation purposes, phenolic for example, it is important to expose the damaged core area, cut out a section and let in a new piece. This is important, as these types of foam suffer a bruise-type collapse of local cells. If not made good, use of the component can cause propagation of the damage to the core due to vibration. It is important to bond any core patch in place using an adhesive recommended by the foam supplier. The adhesive type is important because many adhesives contain solvents that would dissolve certain types of foam.

The localized collapse of foam cells is less likely to occur on structural-type foams, and they do not suffer the propagation of damage by vibration. However, if the damage to the foam core is sufficient to allow sandwich movement, if not repaired, fatigue failure will cause further damage.

Where the damage has broken through the sandwich skins, the widely used method of repair begins with removal of the skin around the damaged area. A hand-held router is ideal for this purpose where the core is damaged too. The router should be set to remove the damaged skin and the underlying core down to the opposing skin. Then a new piece of core can be let in. It is important to use a suitable adhesive to join the edges of the core together, ensuring core continuity.

A patch of the same skin material as originally used on the component should be cut to fit accurately into the hole and flush with the original surface. To restore the skin's performance, a covering patch must be placed over the entire repair area. As a guide to patch size, twice the repair diameter, or width, is advisable.

When the damage to a sandwich structure extends through to both skins, the skins and core should be removed completely. A piece of panel, similar to the original, must be cut to fit the hole, or separate core and skin material to match the panel dimensions. A covering patch should be placed over both sides of the repair. Where possible, covering patches should be of similar material to the original skins. When a hole is cut completely through the sandwich structure, it is also advisable to make it round or oval. This prevents stress build-up in the corners of the repair.

One important point to remember is that where the core material has a vital structural function, it is essential to bond the edges of the replaced core together. If elevated temperatures are being used, foaming adhesive, made for joining core together, can be utilized.

Where the repair is to a component manufactured from pre-made flat panel, a piece of the original panel type can be utilized to form the repair plug.

Repairs are cured according to the type of adhesive used. If at elevated temperature, it is important to ensure that the repair temperature will not degrade the original component. With many resin systems, the original cure temperature can be repeated without detrimental effect, which means that it may be possible to repair using original materials. The suppliers of the materials to be repaired will advise.

Although there will be repair situations that have not been described here, the basic principles can be employed in many circumstances using common sense to make any necessary adjustments to technique. For example, a damaged box section can be repaired by bonding in another similar section made to fit inside. In effect, this is the same as a sandwich-structure repair, again with an external patch, or wrap, to retain the outer surface performance. There may be occasions when original materials cannot be used, or when completely dissimilar materials will be necessary to effect the repair.

Time and experience will lead to most users developing their own versions of suitable repair schemes. Where primary structures are concerned, these schemes will be the result of some form of acceptance test. This serves to build confidence in repairs and sets a standard to work to.

8 Conclusion

This book is intended to give a general insight into modern structural adhesives and composites, but it would be impossible for any book to be a complete work on such a wide and changing technology; changing in the sense that materials technology and supply is continuously making progress. In addition the very important point of manufacturing techniques will also advance with need, that is, the need to cope with more complicated applications or to improve the commercial aspect of any particular project.

There are no definite processing rules or techniques on which to base a complete processing manual. Most modern composite technicians have developed their own methods and techniques to achieve a given end result. These techniques will have been developed from a basic understanding of composite processing.

This book should assist the reader to achieve the necessary basic understanding of composites and their processing. The knowledge can then be utilized as a means of appreciating the make-up of any particular composite structures, or help in making the decision as to whether or not to proceed with some form of composite manufacture, or to establish the method by which any specific composite technique or process is carried out.

The book is also intended to be a guide to equipment requirements and skill levels for anyone considering the use of any form of composite material.

Designing in composite materials will require the same basic skills as for designing in conventional materials, plus information on composite material behaviour and performance. It is not practical to give specific design instruction for a given structure, such as a racing-car or motorcycle chassis, or any other primary structure, where detailed knowledge of the structure and its requirements are essential parts of the design parameters to ensure design success and safety.

Whatever level of composite design skill and material knowledge prevails, it is unlikely that the structural performance of a component will be an exact match for the theoretical performance; composite design cannot be an exact science. If this was the case, all designers, in any particular field, would be equal, and successful.

Theoretical design is a starting point, but making and testing a prototype is still a widely-used method of achieving the desired result. Of course, the nature of the component, or structure, will be the deciding factor on the level of a trial-and-error approach to achieving a design that meets requirements.

A great deal has been achieved in the field of composite technology in recent years and, in many cases, without the availability of a vast amount of previously-obtained data. This applies not only to design, but also to processing techniques. This progress will continue, due to the versatility of modern composites and the people who utilize them.

Index

About the author

Keith Noakes spent almost 20 years employed by Ciba-Geigy, a leading world supplier of raw composite materials. For the first few years, he worked in a development laboratory, followed by five years as senior technical service engineer, and then ten years as senior sales engineer.

A confirmed motor racing enthusiast, Keith has found the introduction and selling of composite technology to the world's leading teams to be a serious, but interesting and enjoyable, business. His close association with these teams and their designers, on projects as diverse as the Jaguar XJR and Heron Suzuki GP bikes, eventually led him to establish Cambridge Composites Ltd, where at the time of writing they are working on various composite structures for Formula 1 and CART cars.

This is Keith's second book on the subject of modern composite materials. His first, *Build to Win* is also published by Osprey.